Hey Natalie Jean

Advice, Musings, and Inspiration on Marriage, Motherhood, and Style

NATALIE HOLBROOK

Stewart, Tabori & Chang, New York

Published in 2015
by Stewart, Tabori & Chang
An imprint of ABRAMS

Library of Congress Control Number:
2014942988
ISBN: 978-1-61769-152-2

Editor: Holly Dolce
Designer: Abby Clawson Low for HI + LOW
Production Manager: Anet Sirna-Bruder

The text of this book was composed in
Adobe Garamond.

Printed and bound in the United States

10 9 8 7 6 5 4 3 2 1

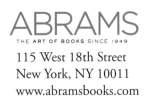

ABRAMS
THE ART OF BOOKS SINCE 1949
115 West 18th Street
New York, NY 10011
www.abramsbooks.com

To my Shirley Jean from your Natalie Jean—
I am dedicating this book to you, Granny Goose,
but only if you hold your mouth right. —TILLIE

On Being a Queen

Some days as I putter around the house, changing diapers and folding laundry and tossing plastic horses back from whence they came into their gray felt toy bin, I'll stop and realize that I feel a little bit like I'm playing house. All these green army guys dotting the floor and the smears of yogurt on the couch stop feeling like a mess. Instead they become the very best kind of make believe. *Make believe this life is mine.* And then I laugh at myself because this *is* my life. And plenty of people would look at it and think, "yuck." Plenty of people would look at my marriage and think, "limiting." Plenty of people would look at my daily list of things I accomplish and think, "silly."

But somehow I feel like I lucked out big time. Somehow I feel like I'm living the dream.

I really like being a mom. Should we go for broke here? I *love* being a mom. I love that feeling where it's just the two of us, and *I got this*—I'm in charge, and the whole day is ours. I love what being a mom brings to me as a whole. I love the way a woman looks when she's holding the hand of somebody small. She takes on this otherworldly, almost supernatural aura when she is about the business of caring for her people. A good mom is gravity, raw earth. She is Mother Nature herself.

It's not like being a mom is necessarily any great accomplishment, and it's not like my life is anything noteworthy or special. It's just the life of a mom cleaning up after a baby. You see it every day in commercials: frumpy mom in a button-up mops the floor. Frumpy mom in a button-up chooses garbage bags that keep the kitchen smelling fresh. Frumpy mom in a button-up makes decisions about the peanut butters, sacrifices herself and her former ambitions so her kids can run wild like ungrateful brats in stain-free clothing, playing soccer and drinking juice and leaving messes in their wake. It's the kind of life businesspeople in suits look down on and

tsk-tsk about, all the while trying to turn a profit from it. You know, "bon-bons and soap operas and minivans." That's all this is.

But this is it. For me, this is it. Brandon goes off to work, and I don't feel jealous of his importance or his title; in fact I rather respect his sacrifice all the more, because I had that life once. I had it, and I hated it. This is it right here, for me; this is the promotion. And Huck isn't the boss, like some might think he is. I'm the boss. I'm *more* than the boss. Huck, that little turkey, is my kingdom, and this place, this tiny apartment on the Upper West Side, this blessed little home, this is my palace. And I will tell you something: It feels regal, the work I do in here. In here, I am a queen.

First thing in the morning when Huck pops his messy head up from the pillows and looks at me with his dream-crazed eyes (even better if he's got sheet wrinkles on his cheeks), sunlight streaming through the windows and the day ahead is ours, using funny voices while unloading the dishwasher, singing silly songs to each other about the things we need at the drugstore and remembering to buy bananas, this is *fun*. It's a party every day, if you want it to be.

I feel lucky, because I had to struggle for this first. This silly life of cleaning up after a baby, of sudsing down the high chair for the millionth time and counting to three for my cooing songbird over and over—I had to fight for it first. My mom always told me this would be the case, when I'd call her crying after another failed month, though I never believed her. After all, it's just menial housework and dirty diapers and negotiating the emotions of a very small person. But she'd tell me that my fight would make my baby sweeter, the late nights easier, the messes smaller. And as always (always *always*), my mom was right. How does that happen? How are moms always right? And it's weird to me sometimes that I find such odd satisfaction in the sweeping. Weirdly, I love sweeping. I see God in the sweeping. I see angels in the laundry. In the middle of sleepless nights, I feel heaven in my arms—heaven that could just as easily have been hell had I not had the chance to find out just how badly I wanted it.

I never thought the day would come, but it has, and I am going to write it in ink because for me this is a milestone: I am grateful for those two years I struggled to get pregnant. I am grateful for those seven years I struggled to find my purpose. I am grateful for every horrible moment of them.

Today. Folding little baby clothes that will be smeared with hummus in a matter of hours. Sweeping up the Cheerios. Hundreds of Cheerios that seem to scurry away under the couch to multiply and replenish the living room when I'm not looking. Stopping at the dinner table to run my hand along its bumpy surface and admire my place settings. A pot of soup on the stove. A fridge stocked full of Diet Coke and a freezer full of frozen chocolate. This is not a kingdom I'm embarrassed to rule over. I rule powerfully here. With grace and elegance and mercy. And sometimes false lashes.

This is a season in my life. This is my chance to be somebody's mother, to make my home my castle, and I'm so honored to do it.

This sovereignty, this kingdom, this is a gift. And *this*, this book you are holding, is about making the most of it. This is a book about our kingdoms. This is a book about being a queen.

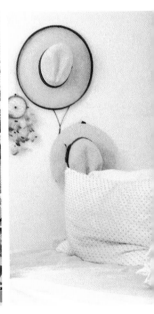

Domesticity Gets a Bad Rap

CHAPTER ONE

My Baby Sleeps in a Closet, and Other Thoughts on Nesting

Well, my baby sleeps in a closet is the first thing you should know. // We live in an 800-square-foot one-bedroom apartment in New York City on the Hell's Kitchen side of the Upper West Side, the perfect little nest for a family of three. 800 square feet, to me, feels entirely enormous. Our last place came in at just under 400 square feet, which is barely big enough to hold a coherent thought let alone all my shoes, and so our place now feels practically palatial by comparison.

I spend most of my days hopping over broken crayons and plastic penguins, sharing space on the rug with a Little People farm set, two plastic pirate ships, and at least ten vintage toy cars from the Duane Reade. And then, when it's time to sleep, Huck and I walk the two steps to the left to the hall closet. Which is his bedroom.

Actually, Huck's hall closet is pretty spectacular. It's the *piece de resistance* of the whole dang joint.

It's also rather large, for a closet, anyway. It's just about five feet long and three feet wide, and everything he needs fits perfectly inside. There's even enough room for his mother to come in at night for some bedtime stories and good-night songs. We like to burrow under the covers, our flashlights zooming across the ceiling, reading books and making shadow puppets and whispering conspiratorial plans for the next day.

A closet bedroom might sound strange, but it's actually a staple of city living. It's also not really a closet. It's a fort. It's a tent in the Sahara, or a rocket ship ready for lift-off. It's the home of a boy and his daydreams, just the size for boyhood mischief. Because the only difference between a hole and a palace is what you bring to it. That's what the city's taught me. A closet, a bedroom, a kingdom, a nest. That is all up to you.

EVERY NEST NEEDS:

1. Somewhere to sit.

2. Something to do.

3. Something utterly useless but very pretty to look at.

4. Something cozy.

5. Somewhere to put your snacks.

6. Somewhere to put your thoughts.

7. And you.

Actually, Huck's hall closet is pretty spectacular.
It's the piece de resistance *of the whole dang joint.*

From the days Huck was literally in a closet. Christmas 2013.

EVERY FORT NEEDS:

1. A favorite toy.

2. A favorite snuggle.

3. A bookshelf to hold his adventures.

4. A spot that's safe and smells like home.

5. A coonskin cap and set of binoculars, should he need to set off unexpectedly on an expedition.

6. A small chest for his treasures.

7. And a night-light for when he needs reassurance it was only a dream.

A closet bedroom might sound strange, but it's actually a staple of city living.

CHAPTER TWO

On Motherhood This Very Minute

I think every birthday, a mom practices letting go. // Huck is three now, the kind of three that drives a hard bargain and knows how to sweet-talk. Sometimes I look at him and my heart skips a beat. He is my proof. He is how I know that I can do things, real things. That I can make magic. Other times I just have to roll my eyes at him, because this child is ridiculous.

Huck can tell entire stories with his eyes. He can flash a crooked smile that has the punch line of every joke ever told. The kid has charisma shooting out his ears. I have no idea what to do with him.

These days, being a mom means loading and reloading a foam bow and arrow, saying things like, "Expert marksmen shouldn't have dirty faces," and retying shoelaces sometimes four different times in fifteen minutes. It means songs wherein key lyrics have been changed to "poop," deep-sea diving at bath time, coming up with answers to a neverending stream of existential life questions, and playing old favorites on the record player for a set of ears still hearing things for the very first time.

Huck's favorite game right now is something we call "Will My Head Fit?" Yes, Huck, your head will fit through the hole between the back of the chair and the seat. No, Huck, it will not fit between the booth and the window at the restaurant. It strikes me that this is the kind of game a dog would be all over. Being a three-year-old is probably exactly like being a dog.

Just this morning as I handed him a bagel for breakfast he said to me, "Mom, cream cheese is the best part of my life. Ever." He repeated the words "ever, ever, ever" with each step he took up the stairs.

This is the most fun time to be a little boy's mom, and the most magical time in a little boy's life. I am the lucky one who gets to take part. His dreams at night are at their most vivid. As his heavy eyes droop toward sleep, adventure still fresh in the flush of his cheeks, I swear I can see sword fights and pirate ships as they sail across his eyelids. Some mornings he wakes in mid-sentence, so excited to tell me about his dream that he's gotten started before he's even opened his eyes.

I love who I've become because of Huck. Motherhood looks good on me. Boys are complete bliss. I never thought I'd enjoy having a kid so much. Babies? I love babies. But kids? I do, I love him in the space he's in right this minute. Grunting macho "hello"s at the skateboarders at the park and squealing with delight at the puppies on their walks. Resisting my hand as we walk into the playground but searching for me the minute he thinks I'm not there. His babyhood just about made my life complete—I mourned the day he outgrew his onesies—but this moment right here is the best it's ever been. Every moment has been the best it's ever been. I have an entire lifetime of the best it's ever beens to come, and oh boy do I look forward to it.

CHAPTER THREE

How to Keep the Sparkly Spark in Your Relationship

I don't know a whole lot about being married; I've only done it once. But I do know a thing or two about being married to Brandon Holbrook, so we'll start from there. // Brandon is only the fourth guy I dated and just the second guy I kissed. Don't even bother to tell me you think that's romantic—I can tell that you're lying.

Before dating Brandon I was with a guy who was practically Brandon's exact opposite. This guy was easy, he was laid-back, he was always willing to let me be the boss when I wanted to be the boss. He liked me when I was bratty, and most of the time, what I said, went. I think I knew it wasn't the best dynamic. It wasn't the kind of relationship that could go anywhere, because while we were very compatible, we just weren't an equal match. I had too much control, which left me with too little room for growth. And then I met Brandon, and suddenly what I had was a classic Noel/Ben situation on my hands. You watched *Felicity*, you know what I mean. Noel is the easy choice for a girl like Felicity. They speak the same language. She's uptight, he's uptight; together they always agree and never question things and always have an easy time with things. A Noel understands a Felicity and always takes her seriously, and a Felicity can very easily take a Noel for granted. For a long, long time, I was staunchly Team Noel. I still am, in a lot of ways. But it wasn't until I met a real-life Ben that I started to understand what a Ben could bring to a girl like Felicity, and why, ultimately, she chose him.

Brandon can be the brick wall that I slam up against. Brandon can be a challenge. He makes me work for it. We come at things from two very different perspectives. He was the jock in high school, and I was the drama nerd. We quibble over the details; he keeps me on my toes. I can fluster him in a way that's incredibly satisfying. We're the Mr. Darcy/Elizabeth Bennet of this novel, is another way to look at it. We are definitely not the Jane and Mr. Bingley. There's an awful lot of sparring going on. Most days I consider it foreplay.

High school me would be astonished if she knew I picked the Ben, but I did. I picked the one that would make me grow, and I'm happy to report I am a whole foot taller than the day we were married. Emotionally speaking, that is.

You know, a perfect marriage really doesn't exist. You could be married to a really great human being, but that doesn't mean he won't occasionally cause you sadness, pain, and unearthly amounts of irritation. It's nice to think that perfection can be achieved if we work at it just right, and marriage advice along those lines seems to be a dime a dozen. Most of it is lovely, but some of it is complete crap. I like to keep a collection of what I consider to be the best awful marriage advice, just for funsies. Here are a few of my favorites.

THE BEST BAD MARRIAGE ADVICE EVER GIVEN, ACCORDING TO ME

1. *YOU SHOULD MARRY YOUR BEST FRIEND.*

Well, you should marry your special friend that you like to have sex with, and maybe keep your best friends as outside-the-marriage relationships. I just figure BFF status is a lot of pressure to put on a guy, especially given the kinds of things I like to talk about with my BFFs. No husband should have to bond with me over menstrual cramps and weigh in on the new pants I just bought. Save the girl talk for the best friends, and save the sex for the husbands. I mean, that's how I look at it anyway.

2. *YOU SHOULD MAKE YOUR SPOUSE'S HAPPINESS YOUR FIRST PRIORITY.*

This is a nice idea in theory, but the truth is it's pretty impossible to have any control over anyone else's feelings but your own. He could be trying his best, you could be trying your best, but an unhappy person is an unhappy person; it's not fair to blame it on your spouse. If you can somehow delete the idea that your husband is responsible for your happiness, and that you can't be happy unless he is giving you exactly what you need, then you'll be a lot happier together a lot more often. If he's in a bad mood, try not to internalize it. If you're irritated by something he says or if he refuses to see reason, you can still be happy and love him anyway. It's easy to feel threatened by your partner's behavior—after all, you're stuck with him for pretty much forever; you've got a lot invested in this—but empower yourself to create your own happiness, and look at your relationship as something that exists entirely outside of it. Make your happiness your first priority, tied with loving and supporting your spouse unconditionally. He's not the keeper of your happiness, and you're not the keeper of his.

3. *DON'T GO TO BED ANGRY.*

No, *do* go to bed angry. Teach yourself to go to bed angry. Learn to enjoy dinner angry, to walk to church together angry, to raise your kids together angry, to love him anyway, angry. Ideally we're all these ultra-enlightened creatures who don't get upset at silly things, but I know I'm not—not even close. Hopefully I never get to the point where I no longer get angry with Brandon, because I only get angry over things I really care about, and wouldn't that be sad if I didn't care anymore? So go to bed angry. Better yet, *don't* go to bed angry; forgive him, even though he's a dolt and then go to bed happy that you're the bigger person. Just, whatever you do, don't stay up with him until you're no longer angry. You might never get to sleep.

---

4. *THE WIFE IS ALWAYS RIGHT.*
Well, actually, that one holds a lot of water if you ask me.

OTHER THOUGHTS

---

1. *YOU MARRY THEIR FLAWS;*
THEIR STRENGTHS ARE A BONUS.
This is one of those times where a long courtship comes in handy. We all come with a set of unique and not-so-unique flaws. For example: I like to shop, and Brandon hates giving back tickles. Or, if you prefer: I can tend to overthink things, and Brandon can be a little callous when he's impatient. It's all good; I knew what I was getting into and so did he. The flaws are the ice cream of this sundae. Some flaws I could *not* put up with. Like infidelity. Or dishonesty. Or being taller than six-foot-three, because that'd be an extravagant height difference for a girl like me. Now, your partner's strengths: Those are the toppings. Like Brandon's good-natured sense of humor and ability to make a room full of people feel at ease, or my quick wit and diplomatic kindness and my good eye for shoes. The cherries *and* the whipped cream, right on top.

---

2. *DO IT ON THE PHONE.*
By which I mean, stage your arguments over the phone, via text message. Brandon and I have been known to text our way through our more heated "discussions" while sitting in the same room, even, because it slows us down and keeps the risk of shouting to zero. Also, having a record of what you've said to each other helps keep you honest. You're less likely to over-exaggerate or say anything too radically insulting when there's a paper trail. Plus, it's a sneaky way to have a disagreement with your spouse about his parenting techniques without undermining his authority in front of the kids. I know someone who records her arguments with her husband on her phone so she can replay certain points back to him as blackmail if needed. Hey, whatever works for you, man.

---

3. *NEVER DECLINE A ROMP IN THE HAY.*
I look at it like a deposit in the savings account. Whatever fiscal responsibility and et cetera. Even if I didn't feel like it up front, I always have a good time in the end.

---

4. *YOU ARE YOUR HUSBAND'S*
PUBLIC RELATIONS REPRESENTATIVE.
As a general rule of thumb, you should never bad-mouth your spouse to your mother. Or to anyone, really, but especially not to your mother. Furthermore, as go-between, it's your

job to manage spousal/familial relations and run interference for him should something come up, and you have every right to expect the same in return. If your in-laws want to come visit, and now is just not a good time, it's your husband's job to break the news gently and preserve that all-important relationship between a wife and her mother-in-law.

---

5. *HAVE A FAMILY MOTTO.*

Brandon and I have been going around and around on this for months, trying to come up with a good motto for our family. So far the best we've come up with is "Holbrooks Don't Give Up," which . . . Maybe a better one would be "Holbrooks: Small but Scrappy." It's a work in progress.

---

6. *FARTING IN THE MIDDLE OF AN ARGUMENT IS ALWAYS A GOOD IDEA.*

I remember it as clear as day. We were in the middle of a heated argument (I have no idea over what, anymore) when Brandon completely out of nowhere let one rip. I was distracted, he was distracted, I started giggling because you can never not laugh where a rogue fart is concerned, and Brandon, rolling with it, shouted, "That's how you make me *feel!*" From then on it sort of became a thing. It comes in real handy in tense situations when you need to *clear the air*, so to speak. Similarly, I once got so frustrated at Brandon that I pulled my shirt off mid-sentence. To-

tal Mia Hamm moment for me—I have no idea where it came from—but that effectively ended things immediately, as it's difficult for any guy to argue in the face of boobs. Most of the time you know when an argument is going nowhere or if it's getting you places, so use these tips at your discretion, and Godspeed.

---

7. *MARRIAGE IS A BUSINESS RELATIONSHIP.*

My mother taught me that romance comes and goes, the good times come and go, but shared goals and an investment in a loving family will be the glue that makes a union between two flawed people ultimately successful. In the ten-plus years we've been married, there have been definite times where I've looked at my husband and thought, *What on earth was I thinking, I can't even stand this person.* But never once have I questioned the future we are building together, or each of our abilities to change and grow as both people and partners. Even in hard times I can look at him and know that I put my engine in a real nice racecar, and that together we are going to go to some amazing places. Go Team Holbrook!

CHAPTER FOUR

Shirley's Drapes

Whenever I do something in my life that is odd (frequently), I like to stop in the moment and say a silent *thank you* to my dearest, craziest Granny Goose, who so generously passed down her crazy genes to me, thus making my life infinitely more interesting by filling it with bizarre and awkward moments.

My Granny Goose, Shirley, is my mother's mother. We share a middle name, a fondness for things being *just so*, and a penchant for agonizingly long and thoughtful shopping trips. She is far and away one of the most important people in my life.

My grandmother loves to go shopping. More precisely, she loves to puzzle and fret over purchasing decisions and pull all sorts of faces and then sigh in exasperation when nothing meets her criteria. "Well, it's just terrible. I have such *needs*," she says.

This one is my personal favorite: "I have to get in a certain mindset before I wear these shoes."

I can so identify with that, you crazy old lady.

My grandma Shirley is the product of a broken home. She was conceived out of wedlock, her parents only marrying for the sake of "doing the right thing." They divorced by the time she was six. Shirley mostly raised herself on her own until high school, when she met Dave Stanger. Shirley was smitten with Dave and his stable family, especially his mother, Viola, who put so much effort into creating a high-functioning and supportive home for her family, and his father, Davis, who worked steadily to make a consistent living and seemed to enjoy coming home to his family at night.

My grandpa Dave is adorable. He kind of whistles through his teeth and shoves his hands in his pockets and rocks back on his heels when you're telling him a good story. He knows how to make you feel like the wittiest, most interesting person in the room. He can cuss like a sailor and wasn't terribly involved in the family religion at the time that he and Shirley were dating, making him the perfect go-between for a woman on the cusp of a major life decision. They were married in 1950 when Shirley was nineteen, and they went on to have five children: Davis, Serena, Paula Kay, Julie (my mother), and James.

My grandmother ran her home like a general at war. Her purchases were her soldiers, expected to perform with valor or else die on the field of battle. She had a tight budget to work with, but she managed to stretch it to hell and back. Her home was full of sturdy, elegant hand-me-downs that she polished to within an inch of their lives, until everything gleamed immaculate and grand. There was not a speck of dust to be found in her vicinity. The Stanger kids were always dressed in full costume regalia, minding their Ps and Qs, because Shirley was also a little bit terrifying. Every single thing she touched needed to bear her stamp of approval, and so everything around her was beautiful and exact. Her SOS pad lived in a footed brass urn by the sink; her drapes received the utmost thought and attention.

Shirley wanted to give her children what she had never had as a child. She wanted her kids to feel their home was a constant, to know that they were loved and safe there, and to have beautiful surroundings they could feel proud to come home to. And so she did it. She did in it spades.

Growing up, my grandma was always unhappy with me about *something*. Either I wasn't sitting up straight enough, or I wasn't playing neatly enough, or worst of all, I wasn't enunciating clearly enough when I spoke to her. I part loved/part hated/part hid from her attention, but even through her toughest scrutiny I knew what she was on about. She never told my cousins to do *anything*. I was special to her, so I got the full work up.

When I turned seventeen and went away to college, something between us changed. All at once, she no longer intimidated me. Our relationship had shifted to something approximating equal footing. Oh, she'd pull rank on me like always, but suddenly I felt sure I could give it right back. I used to blanch in slight horror at the snarky tones that left my lips, and she'd always frown in reply with all her regal condescension, but then she'd look at me out of the corner of one eye and wink at me, just a little bit. She was in on it. I was in on it. We were in on it together.

Brandon and I met the spring of my sophomore year. My Shirley was the first of the family to inspect him, and legend has it she liked Brandon so much she went on to utter the most famously high praise ever given in her illustrious career: "Well, if there's anything wrong with him, I didn't notice."

One warm August evening, when we'd been married six years, and after surviving a deathly boring summer where I supported my husband through his summer internship in San Jose, Brandon and I drove ourselves and all our belongings to my grandparents' hometown of Grants Pass for a quick stopover as part of our two-day trek to Idaho. We pulled in late at night and crept in through their front gate. My grandpa Dave had gone to bed early, as always, and just like always, there was Shirley Jean, up and about, making sure everything was in order for the following day. She welcomed us in, pointed Brandon toward the fresh loaf of bread my grandpa had baked for us earlier that day, and then patted the seat next to her on her brown leather sofa, motioning for me to sit. I sat down slowly and looked at her. It seemed to happen in slow motion. I sat on her couch, and there in that moment it happened: My adulthood. I'd been initiated.

I can't count the number of times I watched as my mom sat in that very same spot on that very same couch to chat with my grandmother late into the night. I used to peek around the corner and listen in, wishing desperately to be invited to sit with them, to be considered a grown-up, to talk about such awfully elegant things, like my grandma's new kitchen rug or what she should do with her drapes. And here it was—it had happened!

We stayed up till well past sensible o'clock that night, and when I finally went to bed it was as a full-blown woman, having weighed in on the state of her drapes and everything.

In the summer of 2013 my Shirley was diagnosed with Alzheimer's disease. It came on hard and fast. The first person she forgot was my grandpa.

"What can I do?" my mom said into the phone when she heard the news from my grandpa Dave.

"I just want you kids to remind her that I'm your dad," he said.

On her best days, my grandma was just a little foggy. On her worst, my grandpa would walk with her to the wall of photos she'd hung in her laundry room a hundred years before and point at all the faces. "See, Shirley?" he would say. "This is me. That's me there with the kids, and that's us on our wedding day.

I know I look different; we've both gotten older. But that's me. That's still me."

My mom likes to tell me the story of when I was born and my Shirley came to visit me in the hospital for the first time. She says she held me in her arms and looked at me, just stared me down all serious-like, and then announced to the room in that lofty tone of hers, "This one's smart." My mom would tell me that story any time she needed me to remember to behave. Because above all else, what I did mattered. What I did was important to her. We always joked that I was my grandma Shirley's favorite, but then none of us were *really* joking. For better or worse, it was true. I was her favorite. Somehow our souls had linked up that day in the hospital, and that's just the way it was. I had her in my back pocket. She carried me in her purse.

It was at Christmas that year that I first met the Shirley that Alzheimer's created. She pulled up the drive with my grandpa Dave just a little before Christmas dinner, got out of the car, and as I waited at the door I braced myself. I could already see the confusion in her eyes, peeking out from behind her fierce mask of determination. "It's so good to see you," she said to me, but I couldn't tell if she believed it. And then she hugged me. And for just a minute it all felt the same, like maybe it really was my crazy Shirley Jean in there. But when she pulled away the look remained, and I knew that I was wrong.

She was just so feeble, standing there with that timid little smile that threatened to break and betray her façade, and it was so strange to me. She had always been so much larger than life, this tower of matriarchy full of this-is-how-it's-going-to-go and because-I-say-so-that's-why. And now she just looked . . . *normal*. Her bravado was missing, and without it she was just some lady. Her voice had changed. All trace of her silly pomp and circumstance were gone. It was all I could do not to cry.

"That's my boyfriend," she said, pointing to my grandpa as if to introduce us. "Isn't he cute?" she asked. I nodded slowly. "He helped me count my spending cash this morning. Well, he *is* an accountant." (My grandpa had sold insurance all his life.) "I just think he's so sweet," she continued, and I wondered, *where did she go?* She was Shirley, but she was not. I wouldn't get away with rolling my eyes at her antics anymore. I certainly couldn't call her Granny Goose, the silly nickname I'd come up with for her when I was eighteen, and she clearly wouldn't know to call me Tillie, the silly nickname she'd come up with for me in return. I was just Natalie now, and she was just Shirley. Someone else's Shirley. Not mine.

I often think of what it must have looked like, the way she might have looked at me when I was just a few hours old. I think of that look on her face, and I think of this look now, this look of confused affection, and my heart breaks a little. Every time I spoke to her that Christmas she would look at me with a funny kind of disappointment bubbling behind her eyes. *Who are you, and why do I like you so much?* it seemed to say.

When I picture my grandmother, I picture her standing at the kitchen sink, slicing vegetables into a bowl, a knife in one fist, a cucumber in the other, the edge of the blade coming flush against the soft pad of her thumb. I think of her every time I'm in the kitchen slicing my own vegetables. I think of her drapes any time I think of mine. I can still see that face she'd make when things were going in a direction she found most displeasing, the Shirley Look, the same look I make any time I find fault with a thing and know I can get away with it. It still makes me laugh, every time I picture it, and now it's gone. It's just gone. And mine is all that's left.

Someday she'll require more care than my grandpa can provide, and she'll need to move into an assisted living facility. Sometimes I imagine what it will be like for her when she moves in. No doubt she will bring a few of her most hardworking soldiers with her, the things she is most proud of, purchases that made her house a home, that belonged at her *real* home, the home she'd lived in for fifty years and created from scratch, the home she has already forgotten. I know she'll forget about us too, about most of the things she created for us. Sometimes I wonder what new life she'll imagine for herself, as she pieces together the parts that she knows as best she can. I wonder what her story will be, what she'll tell herself about herself when the rest of her is gone. Nobody's Shirley. It's almost a brand-new start, isn't it? A new chance at life—a doubtful, confused life; a shadow of a life, perhaps—but a life nonetheless. The chance to create a new story is not something most of us will get to have in our lives, though I suppose, in a way, it is something we are all doing every day.

Two summers ago, just a week after her diagnosis, my parents came into town for a long weekend, and that Sunday afternoon she called my mother for their weekly chat. I'd been meaning to call that Shirley of mine for just about forever, but I'd been putting it off because talking on the phone makes me sweaty, and I was worried I wasn't brave enough. My grandma asked to talk to me as soon as their chat was finished. I swallowed a little nervousness as I was handed the phone, already unsure of who would be meeting me on the other end, but when she spoke it was my Shirley, just like always. I felt so silly for thinking she could be anyone else. How could anything defeat the indomitable Shirley Jean? We caught up on things, and then her voice

halted, and she became very quiet.

"Tillie, I just want you to know, I'm having a little trouble with my memory," she said. She suddenly sounded so far away, and maybe embarrassed, as though she'd done something terribly shameful. "I got sick, honey," she said, "and it's affected my memory. And I just have to live with that now." Her voice started to crack. I sat there, a bit panicked, having never been exposed to my grandmother this vulnerable. I felt weirdly honored to have been entrusted with it, and older now than I'd ever felt before in my life.

"It is so disappointing," she continued, "but I want you to know, Tillie, that I remember you. I remember you, and I remember your husband, and I remember your son. And I love you, honey child."

Sometimes I pretend that was the last thing she ever said to me.

CHAPTER FIVE

On Making a House a Home

These are my feelings on homemaking, so go get some popcorn. // I take a great deal of pride from my home. Sure, the bathroom may not be totally spotless, and the rugs could probably stand to be vacuumed, but you know what, it's pretty in here. There's been some effort, and it shows. I make my home somewhere I love to be not to impress others or live up to some standard or ideal, but out of respect for myself. Fluffing a nest is an act of love and, at the end of the day, a gift to me, from me, *sincerely yours, hugs and kisses.* Because I deserve to live in a castle fit for royalty. And because putting one together can be a hell of a lot of fun.

HERE IS WHAT I FIGURE IT ALL COMES DOWN TO:

LET IT BE USEFUL, BUT ABOVE ALL, LET IT BE BEAUTIFUL.

If there's one thing I've learned living in a small apartment, it's that everything should pull double duty. Throw blankets should be lovely as well as cozy and warm, for movie nights and out-of-town guests. Food storage containers should be pretty. Even simple glass jars. They come in real handy when my husband brings home a bouquet of *I'm sorry* flowers from the deli. I love to spread them out over six or seven jars and place them randomly around the house. A bouquet of inexpensive roses trimmed extra short and tossed into a wide-mouthed mason jar on a bedside table? Nailed it. The bathroom step stool should be nice to look at, your towels should be white and fresh, important documents should be filed away in something lovely.

44

HERE'S A SMALL SAMPLING OF WHAT I LIKE TO LOOK AT WHEN I'M AT HOME.

1. Family albums.

2. Baskets.

3. Antlers.

4. Throw blankets.

5. Throw pillows.

ALSO...

6. Doilies.

7. Hats.

8. Flags.

9. Pretty containers.

10. Dream catchers.

11. Plants.

12. Sheepskin.

WHEN IN DOUBT,
HANG SOME ANTLERS ON IT

I really feel that no home is complete without a giant bit of taxidermy presiding over the living room, overseeing games of Uno and reruns of *Grey's Anatomy*.

PAPER DOILIES

Oh the doily! You can do just about anything with a doily. You can set a table, you can decorate a Christmas tree, you can protect your surfaces from water damage, make name tags, turn your home into a winter wonderland— you name it! A paper doily is the difference between chocolate chip cookies for the neighbors on a flimsy paper plate and chocolate chip cookies for the neighbors on a *pretty*, flimsy paper plate.

MAPS

One year for Christmas I sent my dad a map of Disneyland from 1969 I'd found on eBay that was printed the same year as the one he'd had hung in his bedroom as a kid. When we moved to Idaho, I framed a few maps of our old neighborhood in Brooklyn and hung them in the living room. When we moved back to New York City, I bought a Rand McNally map of the United States, stenciled "HOME SWEET HOME" across the front in white paint, and marked all the places we'd lived with little red hearts. It's a good reminder that home is where the heart is, whatever that means, and that just because

you tell your future husband you don't want to move around a lot doesn't mean he'll listen.

HATS

Hats are the trickiest little buggers. I always end up having a really great hair day on the days I want to wear one. Also tricky is that they can be hard to store. So I like to hang them in clusters on the walls. They're really great in a living room or bedroom—a little bit casual and rugged and homey and relaxed.

HOUSEPLANTS

I think the wonderful thing about houseplants is that they give the sense that someone there is paying attention; that someone is actively nurturing. A thriving houseplant is the sign of a good homemaker. It just provides the loveliest of feelings. I wish I were better at keeping plants alive. (Hey, I've kept a toddler alive!) A clump of succulents huddled together looks so great. About every six months I have to go out and replace a few of the succulents I've managed to kill, but at five bucks a pop it's not a bad way to go. A well-thought-out placement of greenery is a wonderful way to make even the barest of homes look intentional, and a home that feels intentional is a home that's winning.

FLAGS

This is the bad news: Hunting for vintage flags on eBay is hideously addicting. Flags are a great trick for pulling a room together

*I make my home
somewhere I love to be
not to impress others, or
live up to some standard
or ideal, but out
of respect for myself.*

because they're relatively inexpensive for their size and provide a really great punch. A large-scale flag is just about perfect for knocking out a whole empty wall all at once. Plus they are dang easy to personalize to your own family history, and if it isn't personal to you, it has no business living with you.

BASKETS

Once Huck turned three, the situation with his toys seemed to explode overnight. Where do these toys come from? My best defense has been a good collection of baskets. I like wire mesh baskets to corral fruit in the kitchen, and I love the tall, lidded Senegalese baskets for containing all the spare throw blankets and throw pillows and that one fitted sheet I can never figure out what to do with. They bring really great texture and warmth to a room.

SHEEPSKINS

Just about everything in my house has had at least one encounter with a sheepskin. I like for my home to have a lot of white space—kind of an airy feel—but I also want it to feel cozy. A sheepskin is sort of a negative space miracle, where no matter how many sheepskins you have going on, you can still manage to pull off a clean look. It defies the logic of the universe, and I love them for that. I like to get mine at IKEA.

OTHER THOUGHTS ON DECORATING:

A person should only own one smelly candle per smelly candle location at a time. Otherwise you've lost the ship.

You really only need one paint color on your walls, and I promise you, that color is white.

Rugs are stressful, and should be layered for maximum effect.

Respect the personality of your home. Don't overwhelm it with your opinions. If your house is telling you it needs a bib sink, give it a bib sink. If you move into a mid-century modern, get yourself at least one pair of Danish pegged legs. If you live on the coast, you know, let there be a seashell! Your Eames lounger will look great in your stately Victorian, so long as you've been authentic to the architectural history somewhere else. When you combine the soul of your family with the bones of your house, you can create something elevated beyond mere décor. Anyway, it's not a solo, it's a duet.

I really dislike it when my husband tells me he doesn't think a cowhide rug is necessary. Mostly cowhide rugs are always necessary.

The most overrated accessory in your home is probably the throw pillow. Save your throw pillows for last. Don't even consider them until it's the last thing on your plate. And if it requires punching to get it to look right— you know, the karate chop maneuver—you should probably skip it all together. You're the boss: You can make these kinds of decisions.

Throw blankets, on the other hand? Kisses on the face to the person who invented the throw blanket. Are four throw blankets too many throw blankets? You know what, forget I asked.

But throw pillows are a really great way to inject some much-needed contrast in a room, I'll give them that.

Because generally a room should have one overriding identity—be it French provincial or mid-century modern or farmhouse eclectic—and then you should add in a few thoughtful pieces that contradict that identity completely. This is how to avoid a house that looks like a showroom.

I've always felt that family photos belong in a beautiful album on my coffee table, and not on my walls. Every December I sit down with all the digital photos we've taken over the year, save them to our back-up hard drives and our back-up back-up hard drives, and then order a glossy photo album made up of all of our favorites. I don't know, I've just always thought that a framed wedding photo looks out of place and awkward, no matter where you put it.

The obvious exception to this rule is the photo gallery wall. I love me a good photo gallery wall. But a photo gallery wall requires commitment. You can't just flirt with a photo gallery wall—you shit or get off the pot.

CHAPTER SIX

On Tidying

I get a kick out of tidying up around the house. I just like to put stuff away. I don't know, call it a hobby. It's not terribly ambitious, but then neither is fishing, and you don't see that stopping people. // I like to see how much I can carry at once. I feel weirdly proud of myself when I balance it all without dropping a thing. I get an odd sense of satisfaction from it. I like to be as efficient as possible. I don't allow myself to backtrack or stop for any reason; I have to pick up more as I go so my arms are never empty at any time in the process, and I like to get it done super fast. I don't know. It comes close to thrilling sometimes.

It's part of my nightly routine. The house falls quiet, and I buzz all about, picking up toys, thinking deep thoughts, sweeping crumbs off the table, tossing socks in the laundry, throwing away *another* empty string cheese wrapper . . .

Don't get me wrong, I'm not fastidious about it. My house stays mostly clean, but only at face value. I may love to tidy, but I'm almost never bleaching things. I make the tidying a part of my nightly routine . . . and the bleaching a part of my husband's routine. (Or my cleaning service's routine—*shhh!*) And I'm not a perfectionist, either. Stuff can go crooked for weeks on end, and I'm more than all right with that. I can live with a startling amount of imperfection—just look at my husband *(har har).*

There is also the morning tidy, which is equally as lovely as the evening tidy but rather different. In a morning tidy, you roam the house in your bed head and pick things up slowly. This is not a tidy for a rush, this is a *puttering* tidy. The morning tidy is for relaxing; the evening tidy is for speed demons.

AND NOW, MY VERY BEST TIPS ON TIDYING

Start to tidy the minute it hits you. You'll know it when you feel it, and when you feel it, drop everything. And then, you know . . . pick it up.

If you stop moving at any point, you will lose all your momentum and things will start to feel a little pointless. It is for this reason that you cannot stop until the final sock is folded and the last drawer is shut. Go. *Go!*

At first you might backtrack a little or drop a few toys, and that's okay. You're new at this. Take it easy on yourself.

A series of baskets in strategic locations around the house will aid you immensely, in case over-full arms of junk aren't really your thing.

Once you've finished the tidy and your house is smiling at you, crack open a soda, put your feet up, and sigh. Then look around the room for a moment and wonder what on earth you are going to do about those drapes.

CHAPTER SEVEN

In Defense of Beauty

I like to decorate things. // There it is. My home, my body, my shelf in the bathroom where I like to line up my aesthetically pleasing skin creams according to height like trophies—I like for my things to be pretty. I like for my life to be beautiful.

I spend a lot of time thinking about my living room. I like to look at my ceiling and contemplate imaginary light fixtures. It's not that I think that in finding the perfect furniture arrangement I will solve all of life's problems, but sometimes I wonder, is all. When I'm walking down the street and I happen to spot a pair of feet in some really great shoes, all other thoughts leave me completely. I once spent four blocks trying to explain to my mother why the girl on the subway platform in the black New Balance sneakers and the perfectly cropped black denim and a beat-up olive parka with the disheveled hair tucked into an oversized knit scarf could make me lose my train of thought and feel suddenly optimistic about pretty much everything.

I have a weird emotional attachment to my cake plates, and it's not even like I make that many cakes. I put a pretty high priority on a well-balanced outfit, considering there are whole countries falling apart. You know what I want to do when I get old? Needlepoint. I want to sit on a chair with a needle and floss, and I want to do some dang freaking needlepoint. I want one of those standing embroidery hoops. I can't think of anything more luxurious than a standing embroidery hoop. And I want to wear the kind of glasses that come with a headlamp. I want to look like Rick Moranis in *Honey I Shrunk the Kids*, stooped over a fabric rendition of some purple freakin' violets. Back stitch, satin stitch, French knots, breaks for a pot of tea or to knead out the dough that's rising on the counter—this, to me, sounds like heaven.

When I was a kid I sometimes got to go with my mother to a monthly craft night with her friends. Man, the crafts they did back then were ridiculous. And so exciting for a girl my age. Dolls with cornhusk hair you'd twist around a dowel to mold into ringlets. Black-and-white photos of girls wearing large hats with enormous sunflowers on them that you got to smudge yellow chalk into with your fingers. Chore charts. So many chore charts, all of them with tiny wooden boys and girls hanging under their respective jobs, with black dots for eyes and pink dots for cheeks and those exaggerated U-shaped smiles. One time we learned how to quilt for the sole purpose of making quilted toilet-paper-roll covers. It seemed like old-fashioned clothespins were always involved somehow. Nobody does this stuff anymore, and it is such a shame. Those nights were as good as therapy; not a thought in your head, just the methodical application of puff paint.

One afternoon I was out running errands with my dad when the subject of my mother came up. My dad got this faraway look in his eye and said, "Natalie, this is the thing about your mother. Growing up at my house, it never mattered what anything looked like. I had seven brothers. We were always dirty; the house was a constant wreck. I didn't expect that beauty would ever be part of my life. But then I met your mother. She brought beauty into my life. I didn't even know it was missing, but because of her, I have it. It's been so wonderful for a guy like me. She's made my life beautiful, and I'm so grateful for her."

And that's when I knew what I wanted to be when I grew up.

PART TWO

How I Stopped Washing My Hair and Attained Inner Peace

CHAPTER EIGHT

On Being French

First let me start off by saying: I am not French. I am not even remotely French. Which is such a shame. I suppose it is some hallmark of my generation that I so earnestly wish to *seem* French, but there it is. I am not French, but I like it a lot when somebody tells me I could be. Seeming French in some capacity or another is just about the zenith of existence for women my age. Why is that? You want to lay a compliment on a lady? Tell her she looks French. Want me to try a new beauty product? Tell me it's all the rage in Paris. If it is good enough for the French, it is good enough for me, and if it costs me an arm and a leg or makes me seem somewhat crazy, so much the better.

Ultimately, this is why I stopped washing my hair.

I stopped washing my hair because I read once that the French only wash their hair once a week. Their hair is never especially groomed, either, and this is because the French are way cooler than me. It also has to do with the French idea of femininity and embracing one's authentic human nature wholly, in its purest, muskiest form. This is what the Internet has told me, anyway.

It seems to me that all you really need in order to seem French is a muted, basic wardrobe, some very painful shoes, hardly any makeup, unkempt hair fresh from the pillow case, and a severe dose of attitude, like you are doing all of this on purpose and therefore it is fabulous. This is what the French call "personal style." In America, it is also called "lazy" and/or "dirty," and, therefore, I'm in.

An ounce of prevention is the cure when you are French. It's about the prep work. Use good skin creams, and you won't need concealer. Have good sex, and you barely need blush! I like this way of thinking, because I'm really bad at applying blush. As a patriotic American woman, I am accustomed to spending hours getting ready in the morning, but I was freed from the shackles of my mirror upon adopting the French way of life and now never waste longer than five minutes on myself in the morning. Now that I am older and wiser and far more French unto my soul, I am spending those hours on my face *at night*. Creams, serums, eyelash potions, and vitamin capsules—it is all very French of me. And it takes me *forever*. Then, when I roll out of bed the next morning, I only need to make the slightest effort to make myself presentable, and off I go! *Bisous!* I can make it from my bed to the door in ten minutes flat, and here is the best part: Later, if I happen to catch my reflection in a shiny building looking better than anybody has a right to look given how little time I spent primping that morning, I feel all the more beautiful! Because, hey—not bad, considering! This is, I believe, the guiding principle behind the Law of Diminishing Returns, but then I had to take Econ twice because I flunked it the first time, so what do I know.

In closing, I would like to say that my dad does *not* love France. He also does not love Hilary Clinton. But he does love me.

HOW TO NEVER WASH YOUR HAIR, EVER AGAIN, EXCEPT ON A FRIDAY NIGHT

FRIDAY NIGHT: Wash and condition your hair. Don't bother combing it. Sleep on it wet. Doesn't this sound compelling?

SATURDAY MORNING: Pull out your big guns: straighteners, curling irons, whatever you need, and then suffer through some really flat hair, because freshly washed hair is the rudest.

SATURDAY NIGHT: Throw your hair up in a pony and take a shower. Try not to get it wet. Do you have a shower cap? Use it.

SUNDAY MORNING: Wake up, push some hair powder through your roots, brush it through your hair with your fingers, and off you go! You will do this every morning. A word on hair powder: this can be some baby powder, cornstarch (with cocoa powder for the brunettes, holla), or a specialty hair powder from a store. Sprinkle a bit of it into your palms, then rake it through your hair until the residue disappears. I like Lulu Organic's Hair Powder. It smells like patchouli.

SUNDAY NIGHT: After your shower, pull your hair out of its pony and spray it to kingdom come with dry shampoo. You may look like a gray old lady, but don't worry, come morning it'll be as if this never happened. You will do this every night. I like the Batiste line of dry shampoos—classic scent for the first half of the week, and the brown tinted version for the end. Suave makes a really great dry shampoo as well that's more reliably stocked in the drugstores.

MONDAY: You're going to be ready for work in less than ten minutes. You're starting to see why this is so great, aren't you?

TUESDAY: Can you get over how much extra snooze time you have these days?!

WEDNESDAY: You might be tempted to pin back the top half of your hair today. That's okay. Go with it.

THURSDAY: Sport a ruggedly trendy floppy brimmed fedora. Hats are super in these days.

FRIDAY: Just throw it in a top knot already.

FRIDAY NIGHT: Gross, will you wash your hair?

You might find you need to work your way up to the full-week schedule if you're the type to wash your hair every day. Go three days between at first, then four. Add a day every time until you've worked up to a full week. It's worth it, I promise, if only for fifth day hair. Fifth day hair is so great—fifth day hair is like walking sex.

OTHER THOUGHTS ON LOW-MAINTENANCE HAIR:

DO IT YOURSELF

I am having the hair of my life, and I don't care who knows it! I recently started cutting my hair myself, and I've truly never been happier. Nobody knows what I want better than me, and I'm far more willing to overlook imperfections when they were mine and I got them for free. After successfully pulling off three trims in a row, I mentioned it shamefully to my hairdresser friend who'd just returned from a few years in Paris, and she said, "Natalie, that is so French of you. Everybody cuts their own hair in Paris." You have no idea what that did for a girl like me. Well, maybe you do.

HOW TO CUT YOUR OWN HAIR

It's not rocket science.

1. Decide how long you want it, and then make a mental note to cut it a full inch longer. Usually you'll be way off, and by the time you've made it an inch too long, it's actually the length you intended all along. You should never attempt this with wet hair—hair is longer when wet, and you'll always end up shorter than you want. (Remember: It does grow back.)

2. Part your hair in the middle and pull forward on either side of your neck like you are making low pigtails. Slip the full amount of one pigtail between two fingers, run your fingers down the shaft of your hair like your fingers are a straightening iron, and when you get to an inch past the length you want, raise your fingers up with the hair tight inside, and, with your other hand holding the scissors, cut straight across. I usually saw through my hair instead of going for one quick snip; sawing will keep it straighter. Please note: If you have thick hair you'll need to break your pigtails up into even more pigtails to pull this off. Use the just-cut hair as your guidepost for the rest of your hair, and snip to length.

3. Repeat on the other side.

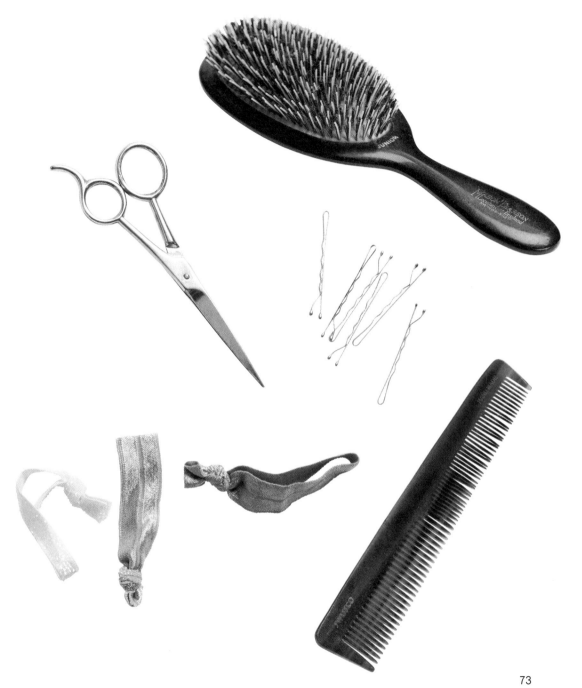

4. Letting your hair fall loose, construct a mirror situation so you can see the back of your head. Normally your two sides will be even, but the back middle will be longer. Using the same technique as earlier, straighten it out by trimming it all to the same length.

NOTE: The shorter the hair, the more tragic the mistakes. This works best on mid-neck-length hair and longer. You can trim your bangs and give your toddler a haircut using this same technique. Two fingers, snip. Always aim for longer. You can always cut more, you can never cut less.

THINK LONG-TERM

The ombré hair color trend of 2013—the gradually lightened ends with the darker roots—has been the greatest hair trend of my life. Not only can it be done in a natural, sun-kissed kind of way, but it can also go super edgy and rocker chic with a little extra bleach. And best of all, you do it once and you're good to go for the next six months. A good ombré takes skill, so do ask around for colorist recommendations.

ONLY BUY THE BEST

Last year I bought a Mason Pearson hairbrush. The Mason Pearson is up there with the most expensive hair tools ever sold. They're completely insane and worth every penny, though I think it's just the emotional satisfaction that's worth it, because after all, *it is only a hairbrush.* I also started using the kind of shampoo you'd hide from the houseguests. I spend well over twenty bucks a bottle, but my stylist friend recommended it wholeheartedly, and sadly I noticed a difference immediately after using it in my hair texture and volume, and I'll never be able to go back to the ninety-nine-cent stuff ever again. But I am only using it once every seven days, so in essence . . . I'm saving money?

ACCEPT THE HEAD GOD GAVE YOU

Authenticity is the most beautiful thing on a woman, and the key to unlocking your sense of inner beauty and confidence is in getting to know yourself, accepting yourself all the way, and then working with what you got, instead of trying to fit into a one-size-fits-all standard of beauty that, I promise you, only works on maybe four people. My hair just wants to part down the center. I've tried reasoning with it, and I've tried wielding my blow dryer like a weapon, but nothing works. It parts down the center. I figure you either fight with it your entire life or else you come to terms with the head God gave you and find peace unto your soul. I finally called a cease-fire on my thirty-year battle with my cowlicks, and good thing. In a cowlick skirmish, nobody wins.

ON SKIN CARE

These days I've been on a personal odyssey

of self-discovery via night cream. Well, first I turned thirty. Then I realized, while standing at the beauty counter at Saks, that I now had license to buy any of the serious-business night creams I wanted. A very dangerous location for such a discovery, but then what can you do. This night cream not only needed to do its job, but also to *say a thing about a person.* Every purchase has potential to say a thing about a person; this is why shopping is ultimately so satisfying. You're not just buying *things*, you're buying *you.* You're buying a defining sense of self for . . . yourself, usually, because nobody else cares. So there I was, wanting not just something that would keep me young but that would also make me feel really cool to myself. And now we have cracked into the mindset of every marketing department known to man, but this isn't supposed to be about serious things—no, this is about night creams, and being French.

In a ridiculous fit of irresponsibility earlier this year I bought myself a tiny tub of La Mer face cream. Let me tell you about La Mer face cream. It is a hack. It costs as much as a yacht and smells vaguely seaweed-y and did precisely nothing for me, apart from make me feel like one of those old ladies in furs you see strolling around the Upper East Side. But from this experience I did learn that my skin is capable of handling a moisturizer of epic magnitude, and with that my skin and I fi-

nally graduated from the high school of Neutrogenas and on into the part of life where we take ourselves enormously seriously.

I decided I wanted to do a lot of research before committing to a moisturizer. I scoured the Internet and popped into department stores, asking all of the absurd questions and learning about things such as vitamins and absorption rates and something called "elastin." The research stage leads seamlessly to the samples stage. Finally I settled on a line of organic oils and creams in aesthetically pleasing packaging that smell a little like dirt and make me inexplicably happy. We are talking *months* of entertainment here. Followed by months of healthy skin! All for the bargain basement price of . . . well, let's not go there. Suffice it to say, I know who I am now, thanks in no small part to Aesop's Damascan Rose Oil treatment.

An ounce of prevention is the cure when you are French. It's about the prep work.

CHAPTER NINE

On Tomboy Style

Artistic control over a man's wardrobe should lie within the wife's jurisdiction—I have always said this. It should be part of the marriage vows. Ideally I'd like for my husband to feel some closet-related autonomy, but the truth of it is that in practice it's just not a very good idea.

The first week Brandon and I were married I went through his clothes and threw out a whole stack of disintegrating tee shirts and outdated sweaters. Show me a woman who says she hasn't done this, and I'll show you a woman with a terrible memory. To make it fair I also sewed up all the holes in his underwear for him. Wasn't that nice of me? All we had at the time was a spool of red thread. He didn't mind.

Back then I found the men's department terribly intimidating. I'd step one foot in there and instantly experience a rather profound stupor of thought. *What am I doing here? Who am I? What would this sweater look like on a boy? Why can't I picture this? What color is this even? These pants are enormous!* Still to this day I can never remember if Brandon has a 30- or a 31-inch waist, and as such I have never once purchased a pair of men's jeans with any kind of confidence.

But life has blessed me with experience beyond measure, and now when I go into the men's department, I crack my knuckles and get right to it. Over the years I've started to feel quite at home there, far away from all the ruffles and sparkles and plunging necklines of the ladies departments. A girl like me can think a heck of a lot more clearly at a safe distance from the polka dots.

I guess I'm becoming a dude, is what it comes to. I pretty much dress like a boy most days. Nothing I own boasts any obvious waistline. I donated every item of color in my closet last year. Positively none of my things sparkle. I don't wear ruffles; ruffles wear me. "Look at this funny person named Natalie I am wearing today!"

I used to love the fancy stuff. When I was a little girl I was very particular about dresses that "turned." I'd perform tests in the mirror, and if a dress didn't reach straight perpendicular status then no chance I'd even *consider* wearing it to school. Who knows what's happened since, be it maturity or changing fashion trends or the post-baby body, but those nipped-in waists just don't feel right any more. I don't feel like myself, or maybe I don't feel like the parts of myself that I like to feel are myself, or maybe it's just that I'm getting lazy, and trying to match peplums with chevrons takes up too much energy. Either way, it's happening. It helps that I got the body of a fifth-grade boy. Aren't you feeling sympathetic for my husband right now?

The best part is, I'm *such* a girl. I love romantic comedies. I do the swoony British literature. (I do suck at math, but that's not my uterus's fault.) I like old lady things, like needlepoint and holding other people's babies. Maybe the reason I feel so comfortable dressing like a man is that I feel so inherently feminine, but mostly I think the reason I feel so comfortable dressing like a man is because all of men's clothing is really flipping comfortable.

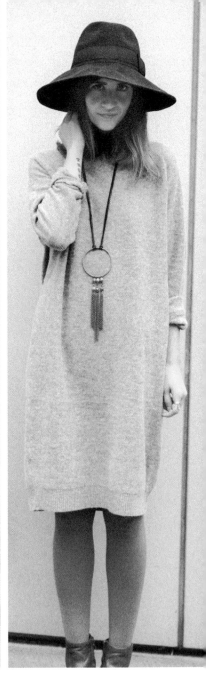

80

CHAPTER TEN

Love Letter to a Uniform

Personal style is such a loaded term. It could mean anything, from a preferred color family to a favorite silhouette to the type of jewelry you naturally gravitate toward. Personal style is just a fancy way of saying personal preference. All of us have it. You don't need to know a thing about fashion to have personal style; you just need to know a thing or two about yourself.

Someone once told me she tries to dress every day like she is going to Jimi Hendrix's funeral. I've thought about this a lot, and I've decided it's a very solid bit of advice indeed. What *couldn't* you wear to a Jimi Hendrix funeral? You could wear just about anything you wanted to a Jimi Hendrix funeral, so long as it kicked a fair amount of ass.

This is a classic example of a good style motto that will do the legwork for you, and you know what? I think everyone should have one. There's just something to making decisions about things, you know? People need rules. None of this "no white after Labor Day" nonsense. I'm talking about individualized rules tailored specifically to you, to your likes and dislikes, your lifestyle, and the kinds of things that get you off. We all deserve to take getting dressed seriously, and we all deserve to feel like our best selves once we're finished. Style mottos are a great way to get there. Something like: "If Mary-Kate would wear it, so will I!" Or: "Does this make me look too much like a tomboy? Or *just right* like a tomboy?" Or perhaps: "I can't picture lugging the groceries in this, and therefore it is a pass." Think of how much simpler your life would be!

Similarly, you could adopt a style icon. I have lots of them. They help me out in a pinch, like all girlfriends do. Mine are Alexa Chung, Mary-Kate Olsen, Jane Birkin and both her daughters—Lou and Charlotte—Sienna Miller, Françoise Hardy, and yes I am just going to say it, Gwyneth Paltrow. I consider these girls my friends, and I take them places with me. The other day at Rag & Bone, Gwyneth told me that the boots I was trying on in brown were all wrong. They made me look like I was wearing a clunky Roman shield of armor on my shins, and *Here, try the black, the black will look sleeker.* I thanked her kindly—in my head you guys, I'm not crazy—but the point is that Gwyneth *would* wear a shield of honor on her shins, but Gwyneth would always keep it sleek. And so, then, shall I. I call up Alexa any time I'm at the thrift store contemplating something boxy. *Hi, Alexa! What do you think of this?* She tells me I look great but to hold out for something with gold buttons. I am worth the gold buttons. Mary-Kate reminds me that even though I'm short, I can pull off all the shapeless tunics I want, so long as I look like I don't give a crap.

Sometimes it's smart to outlaw whole camps of trends in one fell swoop just to save yourself the emotional turmoil. For instance: One time I decided I shouldn't ever wear dangly earrings, and that decision alone has saved me countless hours of accessory shopping.

One semester in college I had a real moment with turtlenecks. It's hard to get any less sexy

than a turtleneck, but that was fine, I was at BYU. Something about my face in the moment really lent itself to turtlenecks, so I threw myself into it headlong and with abandon. The only problem was once I was over it, I was left with all these . . . turtlenecks. Another time I got really into western snap-button shirts and overly large belt buckles. This was the year the world was experiencing its Britney Spears moment. I am talking *low*-rise jeans. I actually owned a pair of jeans that boasted a 1-inch zipper. A zipper that short is completely unnecessary at that point, and yet it showed up anyway. Consider that for your next motivational poster. Whether or not you choose Britney Spears as your personal style icon is entirely up to you—I won't judge. I hear denim-on-denim *is* having a comeback.

ON BASICS

I have a thing for basics. It's about looking effortless, but more than that it's about *being* effortless.

I am endlessly fascinated with the idea of a "wardrobe." Not just a collection of cute things to choose between, but a living entity of clothing that exists as a functioning unit *for you*, and not the other way around.

Take the wardrobe idea one step further, and you've got a uniform. I love me a uniform. I always wanted to go to one of those private schools that made you wear kneesocks. Instinctively I knew that the fewer the choices, the bigger the statement.

I do have a uniform; I am a very predictable, reliable clothes-wearer. My uniform is: ankle boots, skinny jeans, slouchy white tee, neutral-colored sweater, tiny gold jewelry. I get really excited over my morning sweater decision. Do I want to wear this gray sweater? Or *this* gray sweater?

I read once that what every wardrobe needs is a nice pair of slacks, a good tailored blazer, a crisp buttoned shirt, and some kind of pencil skirt. But is it just me? Slacks make me sad. Sometimes I catch myself thinking maybe pencil skirts are a prison of our own making. I don't look all that great in a button-up, anyway. I mean, I have one for emergency situations, but it's definitely not *basic to my lifestyle*. Clearly every lifestyle has its own set of basics. Board room or living room or audition room or hospital room, nobody's basics are everybody's basics. Here are the Natalie basics. The Sometimes Stay-at-Home Sometimes Work-From-Home Sometimes Work Outside but Always Working Hard Self-Respecting Woman-Mom Who Considers Looking Good an Inalienable Right. That's quite the job title. These are my must-haves.

THESE ARE MY MUST-HAVES.

MY BASICS.

1. A good, not-at-all-see-through pair of black leggings. No wait, three. Let's be reasonable.

---

2. A pretty silky shirt for a night out.

---

3. A slouchy gray sweater in one of the earth-made materials: cotton, silk, wool, linen, cashmere.

---

4. An arsenal of shoes: nude high heels, flat brown leather sandals, ass-kicking leather ankle boots in brown and black (if I had to choose, brown is more important).

---

5. A monogrammed leather tote bag. Something you can beat up and it will only look better.

---

6. A personally suited, high-quality skin care regimen and a signature fragrance.

I have a thing for basics. It's about looking effortless, but more than that it's about being *effortless.*

We all deserve to take getting dressed seriously, and we all deserve to feel like our best selves once we're finished.

7. One statement necklace, one statement watch, one statement ring.

8. A leather jacket that makes you look like Joan Jett.

9. A dainty gold necklace, ring, and pair of earrings for the rest of the days when you don't want to wear accessories but *do* want to wear accessories, at the same time.

10. A great pair of skinny jeans, tailored to fit like a glove.

11. A simple-cut tunic dress you can wear with sandals in the summer and over tights in the winter.

12. The perfect slouchy white tee. (Make that five. Okay, ten slouchy tee shirts.) I am not saying this lightly: Your slouchy white tee shirt is key. It is gospel. It's doing all the heavy lifting here; it's the linchpin. It's the very air you breathe! It's your nighttime wear over black leggings; it's your layer under a sweater when you're leaving in a rush; it's your pick up the kids with a kick-ass pair of boots; it's your girls' night out with a cute messy pony; it's your out on a date with heels and red lipstick. Your white slouchy tee is your very best friend. Together you will take on the world!

A slouchy white tee needn't cost a penny over four dollars, though it can also cost just over a Benjamin, if you like. Hey, that's your call. I've always gotten mine at Forever 21 for $3.90 a pop. I buy them two sizes too large. They have about a two-year life span.

I buy ankle boots with a moderate heel and skinny jeans in bulk, and I always have my jeans shortened. When you're on the short-short side, like me, you may need to have your jeans taken in from the knee down while you're at it. Apparently my ankles go where designers have decided calves belong, so by the time I've hemmed a skinny jean to my height they have turned into boot cuts. For the last few years I've been creating my own silhouettes to flatter my legs specifically.

I get all of my pants cropped to just above the ankle. It's the perfect length for every shoe, and on me I've found it creates the most proportionate lines. I'm really big into proportions. When I'm getting dressed it's the first thing I take into account. I like for my tops to be oversized and my bottoms to be trim. Basically I like to be shaped like a Q-tip. Taking in my pants like this over the years has really opened my eyes to the versatility and personal nature of fashion. We can take what we're given to choose from and turn it into what we actually wish were available. Find a tailor you trust. Or buy a sewing machine,

name her Bertie, and get real acquainted with the way she likes her threads wound.

When it comes to jewelry, I like layered tiny gold pieces that would otherwise disappear or overlarge statement pieces that take over an entire outfit, and nothing in between. I like ultra-long, oversized clay bead necklaces, I like stacking gold rings in endless variations, I like watches with faces built for the size of a man's wrist, and I wear tiny studs in my ears that I can forget are there all together. I recently went from owning more than twenty pairs of earrings to just three. I'll wear a bracelet occasionally—a brass cuff or a knit friendship bracelet, but only in the summers.

I just like to keep it simple and let what I do choose pull all the weight it can.

CHAPTER ELEVEN

This One Time at Fashion Week

So this one time I got invited to a fashion show at Fashion Week. // We live right behind Lincoln Center. Living behind Lincoln Center stinks, because Lincoln Center is a *beast*. Any time anything goes down at Lincoln Center, my entire neighborhood becomes a zoo; my usual walking route becomes clogged with trucks, people in all black, and giant dumpsters full of empty water bottles. Fashion Week in September, followed by the Big Apple Circus, capped off by Fashion Week again in February—circus, circus, circus. It really numbs my buns.

Maybe Fashion Week—along with a whole host of other perfectly benign things that I find myself irrationally frustrated with—is the victim here. I'm not unwilling to consider the possibility. Fashion Week doesn't stand a chance against my bad attitude.

The invite in question landed in my inbox the week before Fashion Week. I am not a fashion blogger. But here we are, and I'm getting invited to Fashion Week by a designer I was interested in learning more about, and selfishly, I kind of wanted to go. I tried on the idea that maybe it could be a learning experience? Maybe I would grow as a person? Enhance my human spirit? Break down my ornery walls of prejudice? It would probably be a fun time, and anyway who am I to be such a stinker about things that people legitimately love? I'm not better than anybody. Maybe I've been wrong about this all along. Maybe it's time I get over my bad attitude already and have myself an adventure. So now you know how *that* happened.

When the day came and my sitter arrived, I threw on a pair of silly shoes and walked up through the hustle and bustle of the back side of Lincoln Center. I sashayed up the steps to the tents and in past the bouncers, and then skipped over to the kiosks to scan my barcode and print my ticket. The printed ticket came out shouting "Standing Room Only" at me in

black ink. I wasn't so sure I liked *that*, but after all, why was I even there anyway? I marched myself in the direction of the runway. Now that I was in, I was in. I was committed to the Fashion Week experience at this point.

The farther inside the tents I went, the crazier the chaos became. I was but a minnow in a sea of giant whales, all of us in impossible shoes. The more unattractive the shoe, I quickly noticed, the more likely the foot belonged to the editor-in-chief of some giant fashion periodical. Sunglasses and shoes: these are the "tells." And bad attitudes. At least my own bad attitude was on trend.

And then there was the peplum. Peplum peplum peplum, as far as the eye could see! So much peplum. Too much peplum, if we're being honest. All that peplum serving as a reminder of just how little I belonged there. These glamorous people aren't my people. These are shiny people. Tall people. My people are the type of people to own fifteen slouchy white tee shirts and one terribly ugly yet bafflingly trendy pair of Birkenstock sandals, and exactly zero peplum.

You can't really ask anybody for directions once you're inside the tents, though we all obviously needed directions. All of us who were standing in those tents were in the exact same boat: lost. Wide-eyed and completely confused. Anybody who would have known where to go was either already seated, waiting out the crowds in their black SUVs, or out in the open atrium puffing on their electronic cigarettes. I got my lay of the land as best I could (Samsung table to the left, Rebecca Minkoff to the right, five-dollar soda machine to the—*five dollars!?)*, and then I carefully dodged handbags and navigated my way to the runway of the show I was about to see. And then I was herded into one very long line of very cute girls, one of whom happened to be a friend of mine. "Oh! So nice to see you here!" that sort of thing. This sweet friend and I live in the same neighborhood, have most of the same friends, and blog about roughly the same thing. We have a lot in common, except everything about her is *prettier.* She owns a few peplums, is what I'm saying. She's also the type of girl where all the time you're talking to her you're aware she's not telling you the whole story, and that makes you feel sort of uneven, like you aren't even sure you know your *own* whole story.

QUICK SIDE NOTE: Bumping into someone you know at Fashion Week in the tents while waiting for a show to start *does* make a person feel as though she's made it. Made it to *where,* I'm not entirely sure.

We exchanged pleasantries and some "How are the kids?" and then she hung back with an anxious look on her face that seemed to say, *I'm not sure how much I'm going to tell you* before saying, as though she were choosing her words carefully, "I should probably wait here for my husband."

QUICK SIDE NOTE TO SIDE NOTE: Her husband is the type of husband to get involved in this kind of stuff, whereas my husband is the type of husband whose eyes glaze over if I talk about my hair, but bygones.

I went ahead on my own, surfing the steady wave of peplum and studded shoulders, and then I stood on that very long line of very cute girls, all of us waiting for the doors to the runway—*and to our dreams*—to open.

We waited. We waited some more. I made small talk with the people next to me. I got really thirsty. About an hour later, a stocky man in a black suit came up and announced that the show was full to capacity, and we could all go home. *But . . . I had a ticket,* I thought stupidly to myself before realizing . . . we all had tickets. Easily 200 people already seated inside, and they all had tickets. Easily 200 people behind me on line and *they* all had tickets. We all had tickets, because we all got invited, and we all agreed to come because we all felt special. And who even knows how many others got invited and didn't agree to come, or agreed to come and then didn't bother to show . . . and then it dawned on me, slowly and gloriously, like shining rays of logic in the face of delusional self-important grandeur: We were filler. We were all, all of us, filler. The only reason we were there is because this designer invited everybody and their dog to this show, because this designer wanted a crowd, and it didn't matter to her how she got it. We were the crowd. We weren't somebodies, we were *bodies*.

I felt a little bit bad for all of us. And then I shrugged it off and decided to go home to relieve the babysitter.

I made my way out of the tents, through the masses of very tall girls wearing their coats as capes, as the hilarity of the situation started to sink in. Here I was, walking back the wrong way through a one-way tent, like a salmon swimming upstream against a current of industry types with ticketed seats—and I realized I was kind of enjoying it, this ridiculous humiliation, in a very satisfying, very Anne Shirley type of way. It felt really embarrassing and also *really* funny. So I held my head high and strutted out of there, past the Samsung table and the Maybelline girls, past the five-dollar sodas and the open-air atrium where the beautiful people sat scowling, and out past the bouncers standing importantly at the front doors. I had to suppress my giggles when one of the bouncers side-eyed me with a raised brow. *Look at me*, I wanted to say. *Fashion Week victim!* I stepped down into the Lincoln Center circus and made my way through the crowd of people milling about hoping to have their photos taken.

As I made my way through, a slip of glossy paper was pushed into my fist. "No thank you," I started to say, but the woman was persistent.

"It's a free beauty bag for the first 500 people. Just go to the Duane Reade." I looked at the crumpled bit of paper in my hand and thought, *Well, I do need dishwasher detergent.* What the hell, am I right?

Walking a couple blocks in stupidly silly shoes is something I do really well, just to brag for a minute.

By the time I got there, the beauty bags were long gone. So I bought my dishwasher detergent, and I set my compass for home. No distractions this time.

It was at the corner of 62nd and Amsterdam, just behind the tents, that I bumped into my friend again. She had found her husband, and together they had just exited from backstage. *Backstage, of course,* I thought to myself, before standing up as tall as I could (not very) and saying brightly, "How fun to bump into you again!"

"How did you like it?" her husband asked.

"Oh . . ." I paused. This was it. The epic climax of my Fashion Week misadventure. The epicenter of all of human humiliation, the eye of the storm! I quickly considered my options. None of them looked any good. I made my decision. I chose my words carefully.

"It was great!" I said. Not quite a lie, not quite the whole story. *You're doing good, Natalie!* And now for the graceful exit.

"Ummmmm, I gotta get home to the sitter."

They waved goodbye, and I turned red-faced to the curb. And just as I was about to shrink into my embarrassment forever, a dark-haired girl with a rather large camera stopped me, complimented my shoes, and asked if she could take my photo.

So, I won't lie, that helped.

Later that evening, back in my sensibly ugly yet trendy Birkenstocks and slouchy white tee shirt, my two boys and I left our apartment to hit up a playground.

Huck was in a mood where when he wants his mom he wants his mom, and when he wants his dad he wants his dad, and if he doesn't want you, he *really* doesn't want you.

"No, not mommy!" Huck wailed. "Daddy! Daddy go to the playground!"

Brandon leaned over the stroller and attempted reason.

"We like mommy, buddy! Mommy is the best! Can't mommy come with us? I like it when mommy comes with us."

Huck considered this bit of news carefully, and then decided quite generously that yes, his mother could come along, but only just this once.

Brandon stood up and resumed his place behind the stroller before winking at me.

"It's a good thing I'm around to get you in the door, Miss Standing-Room-Only."

CHAPTER TWELVE

False Lashes 101

Nobody's lips are actually the color of *NARS* Heat Wave, and it is for this reason I decided to start wearing false lashes. // So this is a topic we're going to have to take terribly seriously. I just feel like I'm owed a fat set of Bambi lashes. I'm not very tall, I'm not well endowed—extravagant eyelashes seem completely reasonable to me, and I don't want to hear otherwise.

Enormous lashes are a total game changer. I need 50 percent less makeup to feel made up, my hair looks great a little messy (and let's face it, my hair is always a little messy), and I do mean this sincerely: They look amazing. They also stay on all day. It's quite perplexing.

If you know what you're doing and you buy the right products, a strip of fake lashes from the drugstore can change your life. They take less time to apply than a coat of mascara and come off much easier at night, they're quick and inexpensive to replace once your soldiers get sloppy, they make you look like Bridget Bardot, and you won't need to brush your hair anymore. I promise you, you will not look like you've just wandered off lost on your way to the bathroom at a Halloween party. Who decided fake lashes weren't appropriate for daytime use?

So here are my best tips to properly rock the drugstore falsies. When you're standing in the lash aisle at the drugstore later this afternoon and you're feeling courage in your soul, well, you can thank me then.

I usually wear two sets of lashes at once. If you're going to do it, you may as well do it.

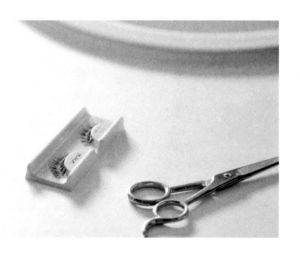
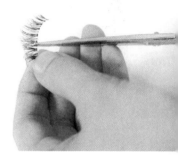

FIRST:

The success of your lashes lies in the strip. Generally speaking, the faker they look in the tray, the better they look on your eye. How is this possible? Beats me. You'll want the lashes that come with a clear strip. Probably you're wondering, *What color lashes do I want?* The answer is black. I know you're scared, but trust me. You don't want brown unless you are *extremely* fair. Buy a couple while you're at it—you might need a few practice strips to get it right. Get the black glue; it's more forgiving. The white glue doesn't play games.

SECOND:

You need to trim these lashes. Nobody looks natural in a set of lashes straight off the tray; you gotta customize them. A lash strip shouldn't line your entire eyelid; it shouldn't even line your entire lash line. Maybe about 5/8ths of it, tops. Trim from the outside end of the strip, not the inside. Most lash strips have slightly shorter lashes at the inside corner, and you need these so they'll look natural. Trim just enough off the outside end that they start about four lashes in from the inside of your eyelid and end just a little before the outside end of your lashes. I usually wear two sets of lashes at once. If you're going to do it, you may as well *do it.*

THIRD:

Apply eyeliner. Liquid is best; a pencil or powder will make it harder to achieve good adhesion.

FOURTH:

Swipe a quick bit of mascara onto your inner lashes. This will act as extra adhesion, as the inside is the part that is most likely to become loose and create lash flop. Please, we don't want lash flop. It also helps to get that natural, gradual build-up to the lash POW you're about to get at your outer corner.

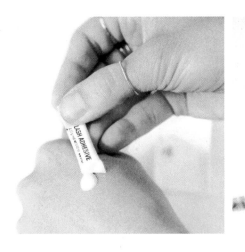

FIFTH:

Squeeze a small dollop of lash glue onto the back of your hand, and then think about what shoes you're going to wear that day. (You want to give the glue a chance to tack up—about the length of a wardrobe conundrum usually does it.)

When people ask you if they're real you can say yes. Don't worry, I'm not going to call you out.

SIXTH:

Hold your lash strip by the lash and tap the lining into your glue, starting at the outer corner and ending at the inner. A little bit goes a long way, so tap lightly. Then tap the whole strip onto a bare stretch of skin along your hand to remove the excess. Hold the strip up, lining facing you, and take a real good look at it. Count to three. You want your glue real tacky, not at all slippery, and plenty of air is how you get there. Now, steel yourself: This is the big dance. Hover your lashes just above your eyelid, and then gently set them down *on top* of your real lashes. Like a hat. A lash hat. On the lash, not the skin. Pinch the fakes into your lashes with your fingers, and push them back into your eyelid as you go, down and back, down and back.

Aaaaand you're done.

PART THREE

Motherhood Looks Good on You

CHAPTER THIRTEEN

My Own Private Idaho

Nestled low among the rolling hills of northern Idaho lies a tiny little town surrounded by wheat fields. Six hours from anywhere, in the middle of nowhere, the town was called Moscow. (Rhymes with Costco.)

Idaho was our worst-case scenario. Idaho was our fallback. Brandon was applying to law schools, Idaho was his least attractive option, and for that very reason I knew we would end up there, because that is just how the universe likes to play me.

I flew out there one weekend in early June to get the lay of the land. As I pulled into Moscow, I knew. I just knew. The weight of it had settled in my chest, and in a way we were already there. It was so disappointing. Grimly I set about the task of finding a job, finding a car, finding a home, finding my courage. Within twenty-four hours it all had fallen into place, and that was it. It was done. I flew back to Brooklyn to the life that I loved, a life that I was now living on borrowed time.

After the city, moving to a place like Moscow feels like stepping off a people mover at the airport. Our life slowed so violently that it almost felt like a stop. It was just the two of us now. Just us two and the decisions we'd made, and this is the part where your real life starts, Natalie. This is the part where you find out who you are.

I took a job at an engineering firm that slowly crushed my will to live. Brandon took his finals and stressed over papers. Every day the sun would set before four o'clock, and every day I became more and more depressed. Clinically miserable, that was my diagnosis. I missed the city, I had no idea who I was anymore; I didn't know what I wanted to do or who I wanted to be. I didn't have direction.

And then it turned out I couldn't get pregnant.

In Moscow, the tulips don't bloom until June. The tulips don't bloom because the winter won't leave. The snow starts in October, and it stays through May, and you dig and you scrape, but you're never really out of it; there's always more coming before you can deal with what's there. There are whole sections of town where the plows don't even bother to show up, and spring never comes and never comes until one day, it does. And then the town blooms all at once, every living thing screams up at you from the soggy, thawing earth; a dizzying spectrum of color. The summer is beautiful and all of six weeks long, and then the clock strikes September and the sky snaps cold, and just like that, it's fall. Something you should know about Moscow in the fall is that Moscow in the fall is not kidding around. You live your whole life waiting for Moscow in the fall. Moscow in the fall will show you the meaning of life. Wading through a sea of leaves at least shin feet tall, cold noses and warm sweaters and glowing pumpkins on every doorstep. The smell of Moscow in the fall is like a direct one-way call with God.

There were little things, though, like on the weekends when the roads were clear and we'd drive to the Costco in Clarkston for a cheap hot dog and a chat with the lobsters in the seafood aisle. To get there we'd drive down the Lewiston grade—this long, steep road down a 2,000-foot drop on the side of a mountain. Ten miles of sharp turns, and our ears always popped at the very same spots before we'd finally hit rock bottom and then wind through the town, a town that smelled startlingly like steamed broccoli. (Paper mill.)

Once at the bottom I'd always look up at where we'd just been in wonder. It was enormous, that grade, so tall, and the start of it was so far up in the clouds it was hardly a speck. *It is so high up there,* I'd always say to Brandon. *And we live up there. Isn't that weird?* Once we had our sauerkraut we'd make the drive home back up the grade, and I'd always wait for that moment when I could tell we were no longer below and had entered the clouds, but that feeling never came. Because we were still on the ground. This never failed to make me think.

One day, I got tired of being such a bummer. My job sucked, my body sucked, Idaho sucked—but it was getting boring to think about, and I just didn't want to carry it anymore. While life on the whole was pretty dumb and underwhelming, every now and then I'd have these little moments that were so absurd, so completely fantastic, that the grin on my face would threaten to crack me in two. They weren't much; they were decidedly unimpressive, but I decided to focus on those times instead. It's going to be fall in Moscow at least once a year, after all. You may as well enjoy it while it's here.

I started keeping a notebook where I wrote down the more ridiculous things in my day that made me smile. It turns out there was a lot about Moscow that could make a girl smile.

Over time the balance started to shift. The big obstacles remained—I still couldn't get pregnant, I still hated my job, I couldn't move those obstacles with all the tractors in all the Palouse—but my days had become so populated with all these little miracles that I had run out of room for the rest of it. The good had caught up to the bad and eclipsed it altogether.

Moscow was such a funny time in our lives, and such a funny little town, too, hardly existing at all once you left its tiny borders. We lived in a kind of suspended animation there, struggling to start, struggling to progress—immobile, as everything seemed to be in Moscow. It is easy to pretend that things have stayed exactly as they were then, frozen in time forever just as I left it: the people, the places, my old narrow hallway extending out the back door, the patio we laid ourselves one hot summer day, those rickety chairs by the splintered barn shed. The grass, the hammock swing in the breeze. The smell of the lilacs. The sun against my face.

Some nights, as I struggle to fall asleep, I go there and walk those quiet sidewalks in my mind. I imagine I can feel the sun beating down on my shoulders, coming up in waves through the weed-cracked concrete. I imagine I can smell the earthy warmth of wheat and pine in the fields. I imagine I can feel the slow easing of my city life as it drains from my fingers. The Moscow of my mind is deserted and it is just me there, empty but for the ghosts of the ones I loved, who slip in and out like wisps of clouds in the atmosphere. I visit my little shoebox of a house on B, the sandwich shop where I'd meet Ollie and Kendall for lunch, and all those street corners where so many of my dreams took flight on a momentary pause on an afternoon run.

I couldn't ever love a place the way I loved my Idaho, I think because my Idaho was never really real. My Idaho was a place I invented, a place that travels with me as I go, like a soft blanket or the steady rhythm of a heart beating slow. It's as much a part of me as any other organ is, pumping courage through my veins. I had everything I ever needed in Idaho; all I had to do was see it.

ON PEONIES

It was the summer of 2008, and I'd accompanied my husband to every nursery in the great panhandle of northern Idaho. His mission was to landscape the vast and barren stretch of earth extending southward from our fence to the curb, and mine was to procure for myself the perfect flowering shrub—a shrub that would turn me into a true woman. A shrub that I could plant in the ground, thus establishing my own flowering roots in the soft earth of Idaho.

Under a sun-drenched sky I pored over peony bushes, contemplating colors and sizes before finally selecting *my* peonies: three in pale pink, one in deep fuchsia. I planted them by the fence in the soft, rich dirt under a gentle June sun. And then I waited.

But nothing happened. My peonies went in and stared at the sun and drank up the water, but nothing. They just sat there. I suppose their stems grew tall and their leaves grew bushy, but those little pink buds remained small and shut tight, unwilling to open or blossom or do anything spectacular. I was so puzzled. Down the street, lazy bushes of peonies would droop heavily to their sidewalks, burdened with their blossoms, sagging with the weight of their easy fabulousness. I just couldn't understand it.

And then I realized that my peonies were taking after me.

Because in those four years we lived in Idaho I was struggling with my own blossoming. I was a small, tight, frustrated knot, full of potential but lacking release. I was a slow little peony, watching the others bend and open and bloom, unable to unlock the secret for myself, lonely and confused and incredibly sad.

But this is what I will remember about my Moscow. Each and every August, months after the other peonies in town had blossomed and faded, my own little peonies would finally burst open.

Three in pale pink, and one in deep fuchsia.

THE FARMHOUSE ON D

There once was an old farmhouse on a street called "D," secluded behind willows and dwarfed behind pine and surrounded by wood where the house fairies and toadstools lived. The roof was a steep A-line covered in moss and pine needles. The side entrance into the kitchen was a charming Dutch door, with a broom propped up against the frame. The front door was painted a fine cherry red. Fallen leaves cluttered the porch, and inside the window a warm lamp glowed soft and yellow. I was fairly certain it smelled like fresh bread inside. Fresh bread and lemon wood polish and pipe tobacco. Next to the house was a stable and inside lived three old, friendly horses, who'd clomp out to the fence to say hello to the passing schoolkids on warm autumn mornings. In the winding driveway between the stable and the farmhouse lived a barn cat named Jinx and a baby-blue pickup truck that had seen better days. Behind the house lay a great grassy field. At night, all the tame neighborhood cats would slip away there to become wild tigers, prowling for mice in the moonlight.

This house lived on my usual running path, so I would see it around four times a week. I always looked forward to it, and sometimes when I felt too tired to keep going I'd use the house as motivation. Once I'd reach the house I'd let myself slow to a walk and drink it all in.

One afternoon I started my run just as a storm blew in. By the time I'd reached my old farmhouse in the trees the rain had found a steady rhythm against my arms. I slowed to my usual walk at the pasture gate and stopped for a minute to tie my shoe and watch my breath gather in the air before me. The white horse slowly made his way out of his warm stable to say hello, and as I reached through the fence to stroke his velvety nose, I suddenly saw it all as though it were very real:

A house dress, green rubber boots, thick woolly socks, and a long sweater coat. Out to feed the chickens and collect the eggs, the barn cat coiling slowly around my feet. A fire in the fireplace, smoke billowing out into the wet morning air, the day's fresh bread just beginning to rise, home-canned preserves and sweet butter on the table. Long afternoon runs and slow quiet evenings, stimulating conversation and good books to read. A chubby baby on my hip. Soothing and shushing and rocking and sleeping.

WRITE IT DOWN, SHE SAYS

I sit in my car in the covered carport of my shoebox of a house on the phone with my mother. It is 8:45. She tells me news from home, and I tell her all the things that have been swimming around in my head since we spoke last. I hog these conversations. The ratio of my words to hers is something alarming, like 42:5.

A friend comes by, and I watch him go inside. The house is glowing, and I can see my chalkboard wall through the kitchen window.

I can picture where my mom is sitting (in the living room) and what she is doing (playing Boggle online) and who is at home with her (my brother Blake). I struggle to keep my voice steady, as I promise to pray for my dad in his job search. I lose the battle completely as I describe my evening to her and what I am feeling.

She tells me to write it down.

"Write it down," she says, "and one day when you are up at night nursing a crying baby, you will remember how much you wanted this."

And so I am writing it down.

I see two mothers walking down the street. I am in my car on my way home from another pointless day in a place that is not my own, and I watch them walk. One is carrying a baby in a Bjorn and the other pushes a stroller. There are so many leaves on the ground that you can't see the sidewalk. They walk slowly; the breeze is soft and not cold. They chat. The woman pats her baby's bottom through the Bjorn. My eyes overflow, and I force them to the road ahead. I am fine by the time I reach the stop sign.

I find out a friend is expecting. I feel jealous, the tears come, but I do not feel angry or bitter. I sigh into my husband's shoulder.

In yoga the instructor tells us to "go to our happy place," and for the first time I don't see myself at Disneyland, where I have my fondest memories of my family and my husband. This time, clear as day, I see my baby. I feel her weight in my arms. I rock her while she nurses. I am filled with incredible peace, even in the cold gym, lying on the hardwood floor, with the weird new-age music.

I want to be a mother. Oh I want to be a mother.

CHAPTER FOURTEEN

How to Make a New Place Yours

When you first move to a place like New York City, it is huge and you are small, but you find these little pockets that somehow, accidentally, become undeniably yours. You shrink the giants to fit in your palm. You take ownership of the street corners and restaurants and park benches where you've been. You create a dent in the air. The next time you pass by, there's a sense of familiarity there. You've made it a pocket of *you.*

The corner of 5th and 13th where we were drenched in a sudden downpour on a Saturday afternoon; the seedy hair shop on 28th where I once bought a bag of human hair from Peru; the little tots playground at Washington Square Park where I could see Huck at all times and not worry if he'd fall; Roosevelt Island out the window of my hospital room the day Huck was born. These are my pockets.

When you move to a place like Moscow and it is small and you feel stunted, you seek out the pockets that make you feel bigger. Once you find them you force yourself in with everything you've got until the pockets have stretched to fit. Pockets of you where one looks inside and sees entire worlds.

I never made Portland mine, because I hadn't figured out by then that you had to make it a priority. I was fifteen, and I allowed myself to be as impermanent as the breeze. The minute I left Portland, Portland forgot all about me.

But I did make BYU my own, just because my first year at BYU went off so hysterically. I flamed out so hard it was a beauty to behold. There's hating a place, and then there's hating a place the way I hated BYU: magnificently, like an artist. But I was letting it get larger than me, and at times I worried it would consume me.

And so I decided to love BYU instead. Premeditated love. Ornery love. Rather than feel frustrated by it, I decided to let its quirks entertain me. And in the process of loving what felt at the time like this unlovable thing, I created my very first pocket. It was just the slightest shift in perspective, just a tiny step to the left, but it had made all the difference. BYU hadn't changed, my feelings for BYU hadn't changed, but *I* had changed. I had found my sweet spot.

AND NOW, HOW TO MAKE A NEW PLACE YOURS—A POCKET HOW-TO

Find a map of town and memorize the main thoroughfares, the order of the streets, public transportation routes, the neighborhoods, how to get to the closest Target. Then, as you navigate the streets, make a note of the places you find and the prettiest routes from point A to point B. Getting past the part where you're routinely feeling lost is a huge step in making a place feel like home.

Try out a few restaurants and diners in town until you find a place that you like enough to call "yours." Then, on Saturday mornings when you're looking for something to do, you can say, "Hey! Let's go to our place for lunch." See? It's starting to feel like yours already.

Map out a few walks or jogs through pretty parts of town so if you ever feel like taking one, you know where to go.

Every day, pick one thing you love about your new place. Do this every day until you get to the point where you like more about your town than you dislike.

Rename a place you visit often with a silly nickname. The sillier the better. There's a grocery store in our neighborhood that Brandon affectionately calls "The Beef." It's a horrible, depressing little grocery store, and the produce is always half rotten, but the minute we gave it a nickname it was suddenly an adventure any time we needed a carton of milk. When you put a name to something, you make it yours; it's like planting a flag. And anyway, finding yourself wherever you are—isn't that the best we can hope for?

CHAPTER FIFTEEN

A Mom's Guide to New York City

I've never been a mom in the suburbs, so what do I know? But if you ask me, New York City is the best place in the world to raise a baby. You just gotta know how to do it.

KNOW YOUR FOOD CHAIN

Understanding the ins and outs of sidewalk etiquette is paramount. Your whole life is lived on the sidewalks, and it can get a little tricky when you add in traffic and bad moods and kids and their accessories. There's a pecking order, and knowing when you have the right of way will make all the difference. Here's a good general rule of thumb: When you are pushing a stroller, the elderly in wheelchairs are the only animal higher than you on the food chain. Always give them the right of way. As far as the elderly *not* in wheelchairs, well, they should get the right of way, but only if they seem nice. Most of the old folks living on the Upper West Side are mean old jerks, and in my experience they're going to give you crap either way. Should you encounter another stroller on the sidewalk you should always give right of way to a double, or to any single that has more kids piled on the ride board than yours. Otherwise, kids, old people, ladies, gents, food delivery guys—forget it. The two-legged can all step aside. Be nice about it, and always say thank you and excuse me, but be firm. And feel free to dispense dirty looks liberally.

DON'T TAKE ANY CRAP

Not from cranky old ladies in line at the Trader Joe's, not from snobby waiters who pretend not to be aware of your child's rights as guaranteed by the US Constitution, not from the hordes of middle school kids in huddled shouting masses of hormones clogging the sidewalks. It's survival of the fittest out here! And if the guy in front of you flagrantly lets the door shut in your face, it is fully acceptable to flip him the bird the minute you make it inside. He deserves it, and how else will he learn? And where are his manners? Was he raised in a barn?

GET OUT EVERY DAY

When Huck was small, we made it a point to get out every day, even in terrible weather. New York City is the greatest for brand-new moms: I almost never felt isolated, because the minute I left my apartment, I was already somewhere! There is so much to see and do right outside your door, and nothing could cure Huck of a crank fit faster than a little people-watching and "fresh" air.

THE STROLLER NAP

God bless the stroller nap! If you can trick your kid into falling asleep in his stroller on a semi-regular basis, you've earned yourself major mom points. Not to mention time to do just about anything you please! Sometimes for as long as three hours! Stroller naps are gold. Not all kids are into stroller naps; it might take some practice. See, now that's my kind of sleep training.

CASH

A lot of places in the city still don't take cards, so I always carry an emergency pretzel fund. Forty bucks should do you, unless you're planning to pay a babysitter once you get home. Babysitters in the city cost more than your rent.

SNACKS

I always really need a hit of sugar around three in the afternoon, especially if I've been pushing a stroller all day. A hidden stash of chocolate is not only helpful for your own emergency blood sugar levels, it's also pretty important in a crisis bribery situation.

BACK-UP SHOES

New York is hard on everything, but it's especially hard on your feet. I always have an extra pair of shoes on hand for the times when I need to be out all day. The quickest way to alleviate blisters and relieve foot fatigue is with a quick change of position. Going from a flat to a low heel, or vice versa, can buy you a couple hours. This is also my secret to avoiding charly horses in the middle of the night. (See also: eat lots of bananas.)

KNOW YOUR ELEVATORS

I love the subway. It's efficient, the people-watching is pretty fantastic, you can get to just about anywhere you need to be, and it's pretty cheap, all things considered. But strollers and subways don't always go together very well. There's the stairs situation, for starters, and then there's the rush hour situation (sardines), so it's smart to go into your train travel with a solid plan of action. I'm not the beefiest of girls, but I can heft my stroller up the stairs if I need to. I just don't *want* to. So I memorized the location and average cleanliness of every subway elevator in the three boroughs I regularly visit, and I mapped out the most direct walking routes to any non-elevator destination I might wish to visit. If for some reason I get there and an elevator I'm counting on is out of service, I immediately email everyone I know to warn them. Elevator karma is something I take seriously. Last year we got a new elevator at the Broadway-Lafayette B, D, F, M station, adding the entirety of SoHo and the Lower East Side to our family stroller repertoire, and I was so excited it was all I talked about for months.

KNOW YOUR BATHROOMS

Knowing where the closest public restroom is at all times is my superpower. I successfully completed pregnancy *and* potty training in this city, and that kind of thing can get you up to speed on toilet situations real fast. You might be tempted to say, "Oh, I'll just find a Starbucks," but NYC Starbucks bathrooms are the Abu Ghraib of public toilets, and you deserve better.

THERE'S ALWAYS THE MUSEUMS

When in doubt, visit a museum. The American Museum of Natural History, the Museum of Modern Art, the Metropolitan Museum, the Guggenheim—these are all kid-friendly museums and make a great destination in both the summer and the winter. The MoMA has a really fantastic kid's section. The Frick, however, is *not* kid-friendly in the slightest. The Met, AMNH, and a host of other smaller museums around the city are federally funded and as such are pay-as-you-wish. This is the city's best-kept secret. Steel up your courage, though, because while the museum patrons are usually happy to accept whatever you donate, you'll occasionally get an attitude. You know, we all have our bad days.

JOIN A MOM'S GROUP

When I was nine months pregnant and out getting the groceries, a woman stopped me at the produce section to invite me to join her baby's play group. This is not unusual. Moms are highly social creatures, it turns out. You don't even need a baby! Just the *threat* of a baby, and you're in. You can find mom's groups and playdates by neighborhood, by age, by your child's interests, through word of mouth, or by signing up for an email list. Having a support system out here is pretty important. I'm part of a mom's group through my local church that holds playdates weekly, swaps babysitting for date nights, runs pre-school co-ops, coordinates school pick-ups and drop-offs, and brings dinners by when a baby is born or if someone is ill. Sometimes a few of us will meet for lunch and just wander around the city for a bit. It's just really nice to be around people who also know the frustration of a broken elevator when you were really counting on it.

GET IT DELIVERED

First of all, have you met Amazon Prime? Allow me to introduce you. The AP, as I call him, is my boyfriend. He is always there for me. I've stopped buying stuff in person nearly completely, and I have developed a really lovely relationship with my UPS guy in the process. His name is Lloyd. For Christmas he gave me an official UPS ballpoint pen. I guess I see him a lot. How did we manage birthday parties before Amazon Prime? I guess what I'm saying is . . . do I sound like an infomercial yet? The monthly diaper deliveries will be your gateway drug, but soon you'll be ordering jumbo-sized marshmallows and henna tattoo kits just because you can, and they'll be there the day after tomorrow. Here in the city you can get just about anything delivered. Take nothing with you! That's my motto. This kind of luxury is never going to happen to me ever again in any other place at any other time in my life, so you better believe I am having all of my toilet paper dropped off at my front door.

KID-FRIENDLY RESTAURANTS

I sort of wonder if there might not be any such thing as a kid-friendly restaurant. I suspect it really has more to do with whether you have a "restaurant-friendly kid." Most places I've been here are kid-friendly, even the places I'd consider a little stuffier; you just have to know how to handle yourself in there. It's a subtle interplay between a child's behavior and a parent's reaction to said behavior that makes the difference. Every place has pasta with butter or bowls of steamed rice, there's always somewhere to park your stroller while you eat, and eating one-handed with a baby on your lap is not so difficult once you get some practice.

MY BEST TIPS FOR SUCCESSFUL MEALS OUT WITH KIDS

—Give your kid his own set of chopsticks and you'll find yourself with a solid forty-five minutes of orange chicken peace and quiet. Kids with chopsticks also eat 50 percent more of their dinner than they would have otherwise.

—At the end of the meal, use a wet wipe or two to wipe up your mess. The staff will love you for it and be happy to accommodate you the next time they see you.

—Statistically speaking, most likely your kid isn't going to poke his eye out with the butter knife, so I always let Huck have one if he wants it so long as he's quiet.

—Download games on your iPhone for emergency situations, and don't you dare feel bad about it!

Remember, if you want your kid to behave in must-behave-at-all-cost situations, you need to put your kid in must-behave-at-all-cost situations as often as possible. And if you have a bad experience, go easy on yourself. Consider it good practice. Be up front with your baby about your expectations, and reward him generously when he's polite and well-mannered, even if he's too little to understand you. I swear it works.

ACCEPT HELP WHEN IT'S OFFERED

Help will be offered a lot out here, you might be surprised to learn. New Yorkers are actually very kind. Moms are sort of an endangered species, and you'll be taken care of by the many grateful non-breeders who recognize your value to society. Chivalry is not dead! Except for when it is, and then it's a nice excuse to exercise some righteous indignation. Sometimes a little righteous indignation feels good. But yes. There is help everywhere. But not from the tourists, though. They're pretty much useless.

SEND OUT YOUR LAUNDRY

For extreme situations where you're up to your eyeballs in things, you can send out your laundry. Your knickers come back to you folded up in these impeccable little squares. It's a dream come true. I know it sounds like the most extravagant nonsense you've ever heard of, and it is. But the price difference, according to my friends who take advantage of it, is negligible. So keep this one in your back pocket. It's just nice to know it's there.

ORDER DINNER ON YOUR WAY HOME
Around ten blocks from home on days when nothing is doing, I order delivery on my smartphone, enjoy my walk home, get in just in time to meet the delivery guy, wash my hands, pull on my stretchy pants, and *ta-da!* Dinner is served. Good work, mom.

AND NOW AS I HAVE SAID CONCERNING STROLLERS
Strollers are exhausting. What a completely ridiculous torture device we spend hundreds of dollars on and then willingly tether ourselves to. They're heavy. They're cumbersome. They're completely enormous. They take up the whole of your apartment. Your home is a shrine to your stroller, and you are naught but a humble pilgrim come to worship at its wheels.

When apartment hunting in the city, your very first priority is going to be your stroller. "Where does the stroller go?" Not "Is there a dishwasher?" or "How's the natural light?" or "Are there hardwoods?" or "Has anybody died in here recently?" but "Where does the stroller go?" Will it fit? Is there a closet or a walkway for parking? Can you leave it in the lobby? And if so, will it get stolen? How are you getting it into the building? Is there an elevator? Can you bump it up the stairs? And the door: Can you open it with one hand, keep it open with your foot, maneuver the stroller inside, then get yourself all the way in before the door shuts on your backside? How do the doors open, anyway? If the doors open out and you are on any kind of stair situation, you are fully screwed.

I always say "We made it!" when we roll into our lobby, like we've just barely escaped with our lives, but this is how it feels. For me, at least. Huck's been sitting there the whole time enjoying the ride of his life. But it's a distinction worthy of an Ironman award every time we run to the drugstore and make it back in one piece; it's really better that we not downplay this. You got one foot in the lobby, you remembered to get the eggs, you've really beat the odds. This is an accomplishment worth celebrating.

One of these days our strollers will come with phone chargers and sound systems and hovercraft technology. And won't that be nice?

CHAPTER SIXTEEN

Huck the Scorpio

Huck was born on Tuesday, October 26, at 1:42 A.M. And so was I. // This is the story of the birth of a mother.

TO BIRTH A SOUL

I woke the weekend before feeling off. It had been a few weeks of low-level, go-nowhere contractions, of waiting it out and hoping for progress, and that morning my heart felt like a butterfly trapped in a jar. I went to the couch in the living room and tried to slow my breathing. Deep breaths in, slow breaths out, but my heart chugged on, sending delightful tingling sensations all up and down my arms.

And so we walked. All through Central Park, up craggy rocks, across bark-dust paths, to lake views and tree views and teenagers-making-out views, upstairs and down.

Brandon challenged me to races up grassy hills as horrified tourists looked on. My body was finally matching the pace of my heart, and it felt so good.

That Monday I waited at the doctor's office for more than an hour. Unexpected staff meeting. Suddenly I felt I needed to be seen immediately. I didn't know why, I was still feeling slightly off, only now my appetite was gone, the flutters in my heart felt wrong, the tingles no longer a dance. I phoned Labor & Delivery. I was coming in.

The L&D nurse looked at me with narrowed eyes.

"Well, you're due in two days," she said, seeming to weigh the decision over. "You're not *really* preeclamptic, but your blood pressure is high. You've been having good contractions every four minutes since you got here . . ."

"I have?!" I said in surprise. I glanced at the readout. The contractions I'd been feeling for days now looked far more impressive on paper.

Then she tapped the blood pressure machine and said, "Well, there's really no point in keeping you pregnant, is there?" And I said, "Well that's what I've been saying!"

I called Brandon ("Really? Really. Today? Are you sure. You're sure?"), who showed up a bit later with my hospital bag and a *Vogue*. You know, light labor reading.

When you are admitted to Labor & Delivery showing signs of preeclampsia (or, as my nurse joked, pre-preeclampsia), they usually induce labor using Pitocin. I'd heard nasty things about that Pitocin: painfully long contractions, too-short breaks between, a veritable marathon of labor. I'd decided to try a natural childbirth, not because I was some sort of stoic about it, but just because I figured I could do it. And I could, I knew I could, but I also knew that everyone has their limits, and Pitocin seems to be a limit all its own.

Pitocin equals epidural equals Don't Try to Be a Hero, Natalie. That sort of thing.

But also I knew my body. And I knew the bodies of the women in my family. Once my mom had her water broken during labor, things went real fast. I knew I needed the chance to go it on my own. I knew I *could* do it on my own, if my body would let me. But I struggled over whether it was something I could really trust my body to do, or if I needed to intervene.

My doctor agreed to break my water and see what would happen before starting the Pitocin drip. And so it was that at 6:00 that evening I became well acquainted with a hook and the insides of my placenta. She checked me once more—dilated to a five and 90 percent effaced. "You have four hours," she said.

And then, we waited.

The contraction monitor clocked my barely noticeable contractions at three- and four-minute intervals while we watched a little naked Ryan Reynolds in *The Proposal* and then the tail end of *Pocahontas*. I *love* *Pocahontas*. If this was labor and delivery, count me in. This was fun. Also those lemon Icees tasted really good.

All too soon it was 9 P.M. and my doctor's shift was ending.

"I'm back at 8:30 tomorrow morning," she said. "I'll come in and check on your progress then, okay?"

"Wait, will I still be here at 8:30 tomorrow morning!?" I asked. It seemed ridiculous. My mother practically had one of my sisters in the hospital hallway, my brother was born in less than forty-five minutes, my great-aunt once gave birth in her car . . . but really? Another twelve hours?

"Well, it's your first baby, so, probably," she said. "Maybe things will go that fast with your second, you never know." Even as the words entered the air I knew they were wrong. I wasn't going to be here when she came back. But even as my body insisted, I ignored it again. Because what do I know?

The new doctor on shift walked in and introduced himself, and already I knew I hated him. I hated his body language, I hated the way he folded his arms and leaned away from me, like he needed to keep his distance. I hated the way he avoided eye contact with me. I wanted to ask, "Isn't there anybody else?"

But after three hours of ogling expensive shoes and Ryan Reynolds's naked backside I was starting to really feel things. Hot, heavy, tight contractions swept over me, and I'd have to stop talking—stop *thinking*—to get through them. I looked at Brandon. *Now* we're talking! *These* are contractions! They were coming on fast, and as I breathed through them I felt alive. Brandon turned off the TV and assumed his father-to-be duties of fanning my face with a clipboard as hard as he could during contractions and spooning me ice chips when I asked. (Admittedly, he was a rather slow ice chipper. I guess he wasn't feeling things as urgently as I was.)

And then, suddenly, I was there. You know, *there*. That point where it is too much, too hard, and you're scared to go on and you know you can't do it. I knew what this was. I was in transition. Or, I *could* be in transition. Because what did I know? Like my doctor said, this was my first baby. I'd probably be here until Kingdom Come. The new doctor announced it was time for the Pitocin, and the room swirled as I tried to stall, tried to think clearly for just a moment. I knew something was happening, but I didn't know that I knew it for sure, and ouch, and why can't my brain cut through this fog, and fan me *harder*, Brandon!

"Can you check my progress first?" I asked through clenched teeth, completely out of breath.

"You've had your water broken; I don't want

to introduce infection," he said, his arms crossed tight against his body, his eyes glued to the floor.

"But, I . . ." I stammered, and then I lost the courage. Who was I to insist he do anything? After all, what did I know?

He left to issue the order, and in the few short moments between intense contractions I asked my nurse what she thought, because somewhere in the few hours I had been there I had fallen deadly in love with her.

"Well, this is your first baby," she told me gently. "You're probably still at a five."

I went immediately into survival mode. If I had hours to go, and Pitocin was on its way, I wanted an epidural, because these contractions were making my teeth hurt and they couldn't possibly get worse and if they did then I'd obviously be forced to kill someone. But I knew I'd regret not trusting my instincts. I struggled to think logically as the contractions tore through me. *Pitocin equals epidural equals Don't Be a Hero, Natalie*, I told myself while my body screamed at me that I was doing it already and it was almost over. But I didn't know what to trust. I started to feel panicked. I was sweating and worried, and I was thinking horribly irrational thoughts, like maybe I was about to die, like maybe the baby might never come out, and I

was going to have to move into the hospital and live off lemon Icees for the rest of my life.

"Fine!" I agreed, just to end the chaos. And then another contraction hit and I couldn't sit still anymore. I needed to *writhe*. I moved all over the bed, swaying my knees in the air and rocking on the mattress. I had to laugh at how silly it must have looked.

"Are you giving the hospital bed a lap dance?" Brandon asked, and I said back with a laugh, "Yes, a squid lap dance."

The nurse was dutifully pushing the first dose of Pitocin through my IV as I wiggled in place, and the anesthesiologist set up for the epidural. "We can give you as many as twenty of these," the nurse said as the she helped me to sit up. "This first one won't really do anything—we'll go slow."

And then my Holbsfanner was sent out of the room, and I needed my Holbsfanner! I literally *could not sit still*; there was no way in all of the heavens and hells and earths and skies to hold my body in place. A startling pressure was setting in, and I wanted to whimper.

"If you can't stop squirming, this isn't going to work," the anesthesiologist said sternly, and I decided I hated him too. And then, just as that enormous needle pricked my skin, I sat up straight in surprise.

"Oh! I need to push!"

The anesthesiologist knew a waste of drugs when he saw one and headed for the door. Here I had just been stabbed for no reason, while the nurse, sensing that something was up, paged for the doctor who walked in the room finally willing to check my progress.

"I need to push," I informed him as he fished around.

"Go for it," he said without looking up.

"Well, what am I at!?" I asked in frustration. I was starting to get incredibly demanding about things, and it all struck me as quite funny.

He took off his gloves and said over his shoulder while he walked across the room, "Uh, you're at a ten."

"The Pitocin won't even kick in for another half hour!" the nurse said in surprise.

I looked at the clock. It had been exactly four hours.

Suddenly the room was teeming with people. A giant spotlight had come out of the ceiling—it sort of felt like I was in the middle of an episode of *The X-Files*. Everyone introduced themselves one at a time (like I was going to remember), and I remember feeling surprisingly okay with the fact that all of these strangers were face-first in my lady parts, until a young-looking intern with dark curly hair introduced himself and said he would be my personal cheerleader, and he was just so sweet, and so innocent, so young, and so fresh, and I started to feel bad for the carnage he was about to witness, so I said back without thinking, "I'm Natalie and this is my vagina, and I'm really, really sorry about this."

And then it was go time.

And then . . . nothing happened.

Where my labor had gone fast, my delivery was like a screeching brake. I pushed for three hours. Huck was crowning for a full forty-five minutes. And every cliché I'd promised myself I'd never do—shouting at my husband (*Fan me! Ice chips! Squeeze harder!*), begging the doctor to use the forceps already, even *screaming*—I did them all. I relished in them.

I felt every last shred of it. Every last second of frustration, every last pounding contraction, every last trembling muscle, every last encouraging squeeze of my hand. I especially liked the part where I tore up the front—I had no idea that could happen. All the while doctors and nurses shouted at me,

Relax this! Tighten that! Hold your breath! Now breathe! Now stop! Now turn this way! None of it made any sense to me, but I tirelessly did as I was told like a good girl would while Huck stubbornly refused to budge. His heart rate chugged on steadily and happily, as though my vaginal canal were some sort of beach resort deck chair. Finally, while silently pleading with God to let the next push be my last, I realized suddenly that I was the one in charge here. It should be me making decisions, I should be the one to issue the orders. Only I could bring this child here, and only I knew how. This is my body, this is my baby, and I know what I am doing, if I can just shut out all the noise and listen. I gritted my teeth. I shut my eyes. And then I gave it hell.

"Natalie, open your eyes!" the nurse said.

When I married that Brandon Holbrook of mine seven years before, I knew I wanted to have his babies. All of the babies in his family are these blond, blue-eyed little Holbrook clones, and though I'd grown to cherish the idea of my own mini-Brandon, *always*, always the babies I rocked and nursed in my dreams were mine: dark-haired, olive skin, with a little rosebud mouth and that indomitable Lovin nose. When we struggled to get pregnant, I had to accept that those babies would probably never be mine. It was a mini-Brandon or nothing. I hardly even missed them, those Lovin babies of my dreams. I was so ready for my blond, skinny baby. I would have given anything for a blond, skinny baby.

But there in the delivery room at 1:46 A.M., I locked eyes on a dark-haired, dark-skinned, incredibly familiar little lover. Complete with mouth and that crazy Lovin nose. And I was floored. My world was torn wide open. It was more than I could even comprehend. He was *mine*. Mine in a way that nothing had ever been mine before. He was mine, and I'd made him. I'd never felt a more powerful, more tangible connection with God in all of my life. I probably never will.

I like to think of those three hours of pushing as the final, exhausting, very literal physical manifestation of the three years I labored to bring Huck into the world. My struggle to trust my body's ability to deliver mirrored my struggle to trust my body's ability to conceive. In the end, I didn't really do it all on my own—nobody ever does—but I felt it all, like I always do. I felt it all, and my stubborn body rejected my every effort to assist it, like it always does.

In the end, it all fell between me and my god. Together we made it work.

And what we made was glorious.

CHAPTER SEVENTEEN

On Nursing

I've been trying my hand at wearing a bra lately. Not for any real reason, just because I figure I should. I have boobs. They may not be much, but I have them, so I may as well go through the motions. So I bought a training bra, because it looked like it would fit. They actually make three sizes of training bras—did you know this? I picked the smallest. It fit really well, actually. This is the extent of my flatness. It was padded, which was gross, but also I was grateful. I need all the help I can get. I ended up returning it, because what's the point? Though it was nice to know it's there. Me and the ten-year-olds. Fist bumps, guys.

Somehow, I'm still lactating. I'm flat as a board, Huck hasn't nursed in over a year, but ask my girls, they're still ready to go. Somehow that's comforting. It's comforting to know that, even if my body won't make a baby from scratch these days, at least it's still interested in fattening one up.

In truth, I loved nursing. *Deeply*. My feelings for nursing reached a level of loveliness that took me entirely by surprise. I could have nursed forever. My goal was to make it past Huck's second birthday, and at two and a half, he was ready to wean. And so, reluctantly, we did. It was heartbreaking for me, actually. It was like the loss of an identity; an identity I'd only barely gotten, and that I still miss to this day.

I miss the way a good letdown felt. I miss the quiet pause it provided in the middle of the day. I used to run my finger under Huck's chin, look into his eyes, and just grin at him like a loon. I was pretty goofy about it. But isn't nursing so great? It *is* so great. Nursing was dreamy. Hand me a baby every two years, and I'll happily nurse for the rest of my life.

I suppose one should call it "breastfeeding" to be rather scientific about it, though the next time I get the chance to do it I'm totally going to call it "juicing." Juicing is super trendy right now. *I don't need to buy a juicer, I AM a juicer!* Squirt squirt.

I dreamed about nursing, starting from the time I was in high school. There'd be a baby, always I'd lose the baby, and then I'd find the baby, feed the baby, and then most times lose him a second time. It seemed I was always finding him in the bathroom. These dreams were tactile. The squish of a baby's midsection, the pinching of the latch—and it felt very specifically just like nursing in real life. Most of my friends in high school were dreaming of Leonardo DiCaprio. I dreamed about nursing.

Nursing is, like, super controversial. Going into it I didn't have any idea how much of a *thing* nursing could be. It was a foregone conclusion for me, something I knew I would do just because I knew I would do it, because all the women in my life did it; it just *happened*. It was hard—it was really hard at times—and it was painful too, at first, but then I knew that it would be. And I also knew that it *wouldn't* be, eventually. I knew I'd get the hang of it if I stuck it out. And luckily, I did. Call it naïveté, but nursing is the one area of motherhood where I simply didn't question myself. I just put my head down and shoved my boobs in. Breastfeeding isn't rocket science, I figured. Only except for sometimes, when it actually is.

But, you know? Successfully breastfeeding a baby doesn't make you a better mom any more than getting pregnant easily makes you

Most of my friends in high school were dreaming of Leonardo DiCaprio. I dreamed about nursing.

a better mom. That's nonsense. Our bodies come up with a million different ways to screw with us. So who's to say that one way is any worse than another? I needed Clomid, you needed formula, let's call the whole thing off. Though I *do* envy you your perky nipples. My nipples at this stage in the game look like elephant trunks.

Weaning was the biggest insult. For weeks my body felt like this throbbing mass of nerve endings. It was like every hormone in my body was invited to party, and some jerk brought Jell-O shots, and they all got blitzed. It was all drunken bar fights and crashing into phone poles and nasty hangovers for *months*.

I *do* know how to do a lot of cool things. My pinkies are double jointed, and I can write my name with my toes, but I think my favorite party trick to date has been the super sly, blink-and-you-missed-it nursing-in-public maneuver that Huck and I used to pull whenever he was hungry and we were out and about. Huck got his best naps in his stroller, and I got my best thinking on my feet, so we spent a lot of time that first year walking around the city. We'd usually make good use of public restrooms and dressing rooms any time Huck was hungry, because this was just The Way it Was Done. After all, Boobs Are Naughty, and Nursing Is Gross. But then a funny idea came to me one day when Huck was so beyond hungry he was angry (hangry) and I was struggling to find an open dressing room in the Forever 21 in Times Square where we could nurse. Side note—if you've ever been to the Forever 21 in Times Square, you know that this is entirely impossible. Only one of the ten thousand dressing rooms will be open, and you can never know which one that will be. I have a theory about this: I think they change it up on you on purpose, just to keep the upper hand, you know, keep you off your balance. So anyway, there we were. Forever 21, Times Square, the doorman telling me where the elevator was, and I'm like, *Sir, I know where the elevator is, I practically live here.* Huck was shouting at me, I was looking about wildly for something cute to try on (may as well make it worth it), when I spotted the single open dressing room. Success! And then we just stood there, on an impossibly long line, while my baby's face got redder and redder. *This is no way to live,* I thought to myself. It was a moment of stark clarity. I eyed the empty chair sitting just a few feet from us. And then I realized, light bulb style: The likelihood that discreetly nursing Huck on that chair could cause any more of a spectacle than all this nonsense, was really very slim.

And thus the seed was planted.

After that, we just nursed out in public all the dang time. I got really good at discreetly getting things done wherever we were. Usually while no one was the wiser. We nursed *everywhere.* In museums, at church, even while walking down 10th Avenue once (desperate times/desperate measures). I was a pretty deft boob maneuverer, it's true; I had me some skills. But even the clumsiest of boobs shouldn't be ashamed of being used whenever and wherever they're needed. We're nursing. We should be proud of this. We don't need to hide.

HERE ARE MY BEST, MOST TRIED-AND-TRUE TRICKS.

1. Button-ups provide easy access, it's true, but I preferred roomy tops I could lift up. A good drape will hide most of the action, and when your baby is finished, gravity will help get you covered much faster than your fingers can work those buttons. Wearing an undershirt you can tug down helps if you're nervous about exposing your back or your sides. I've found that your baby usually covers your front pretty well.

2. Nursing bras are nice if you're a quick snap, but a regular old demi-cup bra I could tug down when needed worked fine.

3. Nursing covers are rad if you're certain you're going to flash somebody, but in my experience they're like a neon sign saying, "I'M NURSING!" I say as soon as you can ditch it, ditch it. If you need coverage, a burp rag or a baby blanket (or even a napkin, in a pinch) will do the job nicely. Huck always hated his nursing cover anyway, so we were happy to fly solo.

4. Get everything ready before letting on to your baby what you're up to. As soon as Huck knew there was a boob in his future, he'd be-come inconsolable until he got it. Reach up under your shirt, adjust everything how you need it, and *then* position the baby, lift your shirt, and secure your latch. (I've found you can cover things with your free hand up until the second his mouth is in position to minimize any flashings.) Similarly, as soon as the latch is broken, free one hand to put everything in place, and *then* remove your baby. Nursing in public is like being on an airplane in extreme turbulence. You know, you put your own oxygen mask on first.

5. Try to find a quiet corner, if you can. Your baby deserves a distraction-free meal. But sometimes you gotta do what you gotta do, and when you do, you should always go with your instincts. Put yourself and your baby first, and don't ever apologize.

Should you need added encouragement, here's this: It's completely legal for a woman to go topless in New York City. For nursing or not. So I say, *Rock it, sister!* You've got my full support. As well as the support of the legislative branch of the New York State government.

CHAPTER EIGHTEEN

Mornings at Home

I'm slowly (very slowly) becoming a morning person. That's not true—I am a die-hard night owl, but I do love waking to the sound of Huck's bare feet slapping against the hardwoods as he sprints from his bedroom to ours at the near crack of dawn. And those last few minutes of cuddles under the covers, talking about what the day will bring and whether he wants pancakes or Lucky Charms for breakfast…I'm getting there. Mornings and I are starting to make peace with each other.

I think the trick is the right morning routine. Something you're excited to face first thing when your bed is so warm. The first thing we do when we climb out of bed is pop our toes against the hardwoods. How this first started I have no idea, but it's really satisfying. Next I steer the boy to the kitchen for some breakfast, and then I head to the record player to see how I'm feeling.

I really look forward to picking a morning album. You just can't beat a good soundtrack for putting on mascara. A little bit of Joni in the air and the burn of a cold Diet Coke . . . Slow mornings at home. Like I said: slowly (very slowly) becoming a morning person.

MY FAVORITE RECORDS FOR PLAYING AROUND THE HOUSE

1. *JONI MITCHELL*
Blue

2. *THE STAVES*
Dead & Born & Grown

3. *BOWIE!*
Chameleon

4. *THE CARPENTERS*
The Singles: 1969–1973

5. *SEALS & CROFTS*
Diamond Girl

6. *BOB DYLAN*
The Times They Are A-Changin'

7. *BON IVER*
For Emma, Forever Ago

8. *JANE BIRKIN & SERGE GAINSBOURG*
Je T'Aime . . . Moi Non Plus

9. *CAROLE KING*
Tapestry

10. *DIONNE WARWICK*
The Very Best of Dionne Warwick

11. *COLTRANE*
Any Coltrane will work

12. *THE SOUND OF MUSIC*
Soundtrack (come on, you know you love it)

13. *SIMON & GARFUNKEL*
Bookends

14. *POINTER SISTERS*
Break Out

CHAPTER NINETEEN

On Grooves

Our record player is a piece of crap. It was an impulse purchase one afternoon when I was running through the Target accomplishing absolutely nothing of importance. // I started to notice pretty quickly that certain records were skipping in certain spots. It was a fun little mystery, and after consulting my friend The Google, I discovered there was something off in the weight of the arm, causing the needle to jump out of its groove, especially during crescendos. Turns out all I needed was a penny and all would be restored. Actually, ours required a quarter, but nevertheless, a little extra weight was all it took to keep our needle in its groove. And then I got really excited about this, because I like to think in analogies. Like Jesus.

Over the summer a few years ago my husband had a bit of a nervous breakdown. He totally cracked, is what happened. Tough clients at work and mounting pressures, and things had suddenly become overwhelming. He felt like a failure; he worried he wasn't good enough. What was once a job he enjoyed and could do without much effort suddenly seemed frightening and impossible. Even simple things like sending a quick email had become unmanageable. I suspected something was up when he became more short-tempered than usual, but I really knew it was serious when he started coming home unexpectedly in the middle of the day. I had the thought to lightheartedly joke that he couldn't quit his job without talking to me first, and good thing I did, because one day soon after that he "came home early" at ten in the morning. We hadn't even brushed our teeth yet and there he was, sitting on the bed, his eyes wild, telling me he was going to quit his job that afternoon, but, as promised, he was here to tell me first.

I remember thinking, *Well, this is it.* This was the exact moment in time when I became a real wife, in the real, grown-up, till-death-do-us-part sense of the word. He wasn't thinking clearly. I could see it in his eyes—the months of tension built up and screaming to get out. I knew in that moment that I had to pull it together for us both.

The hours that followed were some of the most tense hours of my life. He needed to quit his job and saw it as a personal offense that I wouldn't agree with him. But I wasn't going to let him self-destruct. Slowly, I got him to see that it wasn't about his job at all. This wasn't a career crisis. He was having an anxiety attack, a big one, and what he really needed was a break, maybe a little help, but definitely, more than anything, what he needed was a reset back to reality. He needed to get back in his groove.

Brandon took a bit of a sabbatical from work on medical leave to recover and regroup. He flew to Utah to visit his parents and hike up some mountains. He spent a lot of time at the playgrounds with Huck. He read books and talked to counselors. By and by, his heartbeat returned to normal, his job became enjoyable again, and normal life resumed. But one night, while he was still in the thick of it, we sat together on the couch, our legs wrapped up in each other's like some kind of pretzel, and had ourselves a really good talk about things.

So I guess I'm used to getting my needle knocked out of its groove. The music of my life is an erratic mix of crescendos and staccatos and spastic drum solos. Time and time again I get the wind knocked out of me, and time and time again I stop in my tracks and raise my needle, assess the situation, and jump back in it. Because you always have to jump back in it. But what was second nature to me was an entirely new experience for Brandon. If I am the drums, my husband is more of an upright bass. He's steady and stable, always keeping the beat. Getting knocked out isn't something that happens often for a guy like Brandon, but when it does, the process of resetting is exactly the same.

You just have to find your groove. Find your place in it, hold on like hell, and ride it out. And when life gets loud and you're knocked clean out, that's okay. Reassess, readjust, find your penny—maybe you need a quarter. Just find yourself in it and make it yours, and then hop right back to it.

HOW TO BEAT THE BLAHS

I lead a pretty charmed life, I do. I have a handsome husband. He drives me crazy, and sometimes I really want to call his mother and tell on him (she'd just take his side), but there is nothing that makes me happier than when I can make him laugh. Watching him be a father is the sexiest thing I've ever seen, and also he grows this gorgeous thick orange beard that makes my heart all fluttery, so I guess it works out. I have a really great kid.

I don't even *like* kids, and I like this kid. He is the pomegranate on my Christmas wreath, and I tell you what, being his mom has been rad. I live in New York City; I *love* New York City! New York is kind of this bizarre other-world where stupidly fun things happen all the time, and I'm really lucky. I know I'm really lucky. I walk around most days feeling really pretty great. Absurdly happy, even. It's gross. But it wasn't always this good, and if we're going to be honest with each other, even when life is at its best it's easy for me to find myself in a funk. Because nothing can *make* a person happy. It's the person that makes the happy.

I have a lot of experience in beating The Blahs. We all do; we all get The Blahs. No set of circumstances can keep them away for too long, not even the best of circumstances. But I've figured out how to beat them, kind of like a cheat in Super Mario Bros. that gets you to the end a little quicker, and here is what I do.

---

1. I get myself ready for the day, every day. No matter what. From lipstick to socks, because staying in pajamas all day is the broken window of my soul, inviting in all of the squatters. I also make the bed, pillows fluffed. You know, nothing makes a day feel more pointless than crawling back into an unmade bed at the end of it.

---

2. Getting out of the house for a bit of fresh air has a way of clearing through even the thickest cobwebs of doom. It's easy to hole up when you're in a bad mood, and it's even easier to think you're doing the world at large a favor by staying in, but the truth is, three gulps of outside air and you'll feel at least 300 percent better. I like to go out for a Diet Coke and then come up with ridiculous things to do while I'm drinking it. You know when you have a moment with the dog in the window of the house you just drove past? Sometimes I do that on purpose. Some mornings I have to scour the cupboards for an excuse to run to the store to pick up some random item I probably don't need now but could conceivably need in the somewhat near future. Are you running out of toilet paper? I think your baking soda is almost expired. Sometimes this leads to having one too many tubes of toothpaste in the bathroom, but such is life.

---

3. I believe in the power of a real good dance party in the car. But you gotta turn the music up really, really loud—so loud that it drowns everything else and pushes every last bad thought out of your body until all you are is sound.

---

4. Stand facing the sun with your eyes shut tight until your eyelids glow red.

---

5. Tackle some meaningless project. The more meaningless the better. Sometimes this involves painting your bathroom; usually it's just a matter of looking through your sock drawer.

---

6. Go outside and see how fast you can walk. My mother used to compete in speed walking tournaments. She had a special pair of shoes made for it and everything. One afternoon she taught me the proper way to do it—it's completely ridiculous. The rules are you must keep one foot on the ground at all times, and the trick of this is in getting your one leg out of your other leg's way as quickly as possible. (There is definitely a metaphor in this.) To get to real high speeds you have to wiggle your hips side to side in this comical, duckish manner, with your arms snapped to your sides like a T. rex. And then you pump them like the wheels of a train. No bad mood can carry on through this kind of ordeal. Try it.

---

7. Put on *You've Got Mail* and cry through the whole thing. Come on. Zip zip.

---

8. Find a puppy. Touch your forehead to his while you scratch behind his ears, then bury your face in his belly.

---

9. Decide The Blahs are worth reveling in, and give yourself ten minutes to completely wallow. Just *bask* in it. Get as close to the bottom of it as possible and discover what's there.

And if you can fix it, fix it. And if you can't fix it, go do some jumping jacks or Google a knock-knock joke.

---

10. Put on a hat. It's nearly impossible to feel sad when you're wearing a hat.

---

11. Remind yourself that The Blahs are like a tunnel. And you will get to the end. You won't just *see* the light at the end of the tunnel, you'll be *at* the light at the end of the tunnel. We're all *in* the tunnel, because nobody ever really leaves the tunnel . . . Well, that sounds grim. What I mean to say is, nobody ever gets far enough outside the tunnel that they can't accidentally stumble back in. So every moment that feels better than the last? That's a victory. Set your expectations realistically. Don't expect to get there today. Just expect *one step closer.* Every day your tunnel will be shorter and the light a little brighter.

---

12. Sometimes people will tell you to take it one day at a time. They mean well, and that might very well work for some, but I like to take it one life at a time. I imagine myself in the future, when I've beaten this thing. What will I look like then? What sorts of things am I doing, and how do I feel? What am I wearing? And then I try and figure out what all I did to get there. What was the trick? Where did it start, and how can I start now? I like to imagine myself old and gray, sitting peaceful-ly in a chair (it is covered in doilies), thinking back to this exact moment in my life. How will I feel about it? I'll feel tender and sympathetic, I'm sure, because I'm a nice person and because this is hard, but won't I also feel a little regret for every moment I gave it? Can I use that future regret to change my focus now, even ever so slightly? I like to imagine myself in the earth. Decomposing. Rotting. Worms and stuff. By that time, no doubt, I'll have faced and conquered far worse than this. I'll have loved and lost and owned a lot of really great shoes. I'll be at peace then, whether I am at peace right now or not. And will this have mattered much? Will this be a defin-ing struggle? Or just a blip? Will I want *this* in the ground with me? I like to picture heaven, where my soul is freed from silly things, and I no longer have cankles. And then I imagine God, in the present, next to me. Sitting shiva for my struggles. Mourning. He is quiet and still, His hands in his lap, but His love radi-ates onto me in waves. I can see them. Visible waves. I think they're kind of a marigold col-or. Don't you think marigold is the most fan-tastic name for a color? Then I picture Huck when he was three days old. There is nothing that Huck at three days old can't fix. I stop and think about what it was like to hold him. How his eyes fluttered, how his fingers curled around the air, the little weight of his body, the curve of his spine, his tiny bottom in the palm of my hand. There is something so calm about the space surrounding a newborn, with God still so fresh on their skin, that immediately resets my perspective. Every time.

It is a daily task to stop and remind myself that whether or not this season of life is particularly difficult, it is still just a season. I am always surrounded by a beauty that I can choose to focus on instead. Even in pain, there are moments I'll remember with fondness, experiences I'll take to my grave with pride. This is it. Right now. And even if the happiness I make for myself today is so silly and insignificant, it counts. And I'll be so grateful that I paid attention.

As my husband likes to say, "You are only dust." Only earth, only clay, no different in the end from the moss or the trees. "Consider the lilies of the field," he said to me once, which made me sigh so loud the neighbors could hear it. He's right, of course. He's always right. "Brandon is right"—I'm going to have that tattooed on my arm so I will stop forgetting. Brandon is right. We are only dust.

But the dust built the pyramids, you know.

And even if the happiness I make for myself today is so silly and insignificant, it counts. And I'll be so grateful that I paid attention.

CHAPTER TWENTY

What Would Meg Ryan Do?
A Quick Manifesto on Femininity

I spend a disproportionate amount of time watching Meg Ryan movies. *When Harry Met Mail in Seattle*, is what I like to call them. The Holy Trilogy of the Church of Nora Ephron.

Dear Friend,

I like to start my notes to you as if we're already in the middle of a conversation. I pretend we are the oldest and dearest friends, as opposed to what we actually are: people who don't know each other's names and met in a chat room where we'd both claimed we'd never been before. What will NY152 say today, *I wonder. I turn on my computer, I wait impatiently as it connects, I go online, and my breath catches in my chest until I hear three little words: You've got mail. I hear nothing, not even a sound on the streets of New York, just the beat of my own heart. I have mail. From you.*

I like *When Harry Met Sally* for when I am feeling cerebral, I like *You've Got Mail* for when I am feeling emotional, I like *Sleepless*

in Seattle on the off day when I just really need to recite the "shriveled little legs" scene. (Also, I just want to say—though it's not a work of Ms. Ephron's—*French Kiss* is a highly underrated bit of cinematic brilliance. Kevin Klein is surprisingly hot, and, in closing, *lactose intoleraaaaaaaaance!*)

On my best of days, I like to imagine I am living in a Nora Ephron film. On my worst of days too. I think a little bit like maybe Nora's Meg is my fairy godmother. She might be all of our fairy godmothers, come to think of it. I am a proud member of the Nora Ephron tribe, we who love doilies and babies and expect to be taken seriously in spite of it. (Or maybe *because* of it.) It's just like Sam said to Dr. Marcia Fieldstone about his deceased wife: "She made everything beautiful."

AND NOW, THE MEG RYAN GUIDE TO LIFE AND LOVE, ACCORDING TO NATALIE HOLBROOK

1. *HANG UP MORE TWINKLE LIGHTS.*
And get the eucalyptus candles; they make your apartment smell mossy.

2. *GO TO THE MATTRESSES.*
Fight. Fight to the death! Fly to France to get him back! Do not leave that lobby until you are good and ready!

3. *SLAP HIM AT A WEDDING.*
You are not a consolation prize. Is one of us supposed to be a dog in this scenario!?

4. *GET IT ON THE SIDE.*
On the side is a very big thing for you. You want the pie a la mode, but only if it's heated. And not on the top; you want it on the side. And if there is no ice cream, you want whipped cream, on the top, but only if it is real whipped cream; if it is from a can then nothing.

5. *EXPECT TO GET TO CUDDLE.*
You are not the one with the problem here.

6. *BE PRACTICAL.*
Women are very practical, even Ingrid Bergman, which is why she gets on the plane at the end of the movie.

7. *FEEL ALL OF THE FEELINGS.*
The big red bow! They're making the album! I bet your sentimental heart beats wildly over whether or not that Mr. Darcy and oh, what's her name . . . Elizabeth Bennet, are really going to get together.

8. *RELISH THE DETAILS.*
Words like thither. Mischance. Felicity. Don't you love the smell of Scotch tape?

9. *TAKE CARE OF YOURSELF.*
Go get a manicure and forget to vote.

10. *SING IN THE CAR.*
Harses harses harses harses.

11. *ALWAYS REMEMBER YOUR MANNERS.*
That caviar is a garnish!

12. *WHATEVER ELSE ANYTHING IS, IT OUGHT TO BEGIN BY BEING PERSONAL.*
What is so wrong with being personal?

CHAPTER TWENTY-ONE

On Babies

The first time I was infertile, it was 2007. That was an especially fun time for me. The first time I thought about babies, in any wanting-one kind of way, *that* was in 2005. It was a commercial for apple juice, at three in the afternoon, on a Saturday in February.

I was sitting on the brown couch in the living room of our apartment in Brooklyn Heights, I was probably eating a bowl of Cheerios, and the commercial started with a mom in a grocery store pushing a cart through the produce aisle. She's got a chubby baby sitting in the cart. She wanders slowly past the fruit, she's pondering deeply the intricacies of life, as you do in the produce aisle, when she comes to a pile of apples with a sign out the top that says "Made from Concentrate." Mom is clearly not impressed with this turn of events, so she pushes the cart a little bit farther to the next pile of apples, which is actually a pile of apple juices, but that's not the point, because the point is that the mom leans in just a little and gives her baby a bit of a coo. It was probably a very strategic coo, directed by marketing types trying to get me to trust this lady's judgment, but bygones. The baby smiles back and kicks its chubby legs, and that was it. POW. Done for. I remember I sort of sat there for a moment, frozen in time, my spoon hovering mid-bite while apple juice poured from somewhere off screen into the glass on TV, and I said to Brandon, who was brushing his teeth in the bathroom, *Hey! I think I want one of those!*

Well, it wasn't so much that I wanted a baby, more like I wanted to shove its whole fat thigh into my mouth all at once. Shoot, somebody done turned on my baby factory.

It was another seven years until a baby finally kicked its chubby legs in my own grocery cart. And doesn't that seem excessive?

The first time I was infertile, it was 2007. Well, I'm not *infertile,* I just needed an assist. A Stockton to my Malone. A Robin to my Batman. A Jacob Black to my Bella Swan. Something like that.

Trying for a baby is fun for about ten minutes. Pretty soon it's all stress and timing and legs in the air, thinking everything is a pregnancy symptom, getting your hopes up so high and then feeling miserable when it lets you down. This is no way to live a life.

It took me a long time and a lot of unhelpful doctors before I discovered what was happening. Turns out my body doesn't produce enough hormones at the back end of my cycle to sustain a pregnancy. It's called a Luteal Phase Deficiency, and it's when the space between ovulation and menses is fewer than twelve days. My cycle likes to give me about ten to work with, and sometimes in those last few days I feel a little bit pregnant, but then, I'm not. It's not possible to be all the way pregnant with bottoming-out hormones all the time. This is not to say I'll never get pregnant on my own—hormones are confusing little buggers—but it *is* to say it's not terribly likely.

And then, seven years after I decided I wanted one, I got one. Thanks to a nine-dollar prescription that I picked up at the Walmart for Clomid. God bless Clomid. Amen.

I was a little bit terrified of the Clomid, I admit. But it turns out it's not so bad, so long as you have a plan of attack.

AND NOW, HOW TO SURVIVE THE CLOMID (In Five Easy Steps)

1. Whenever you feel dizzy, or crabby, or if ever you have a hot flash—*you will*—sing out "Clooooo-miiiiiid" in a high operatic voice as loudly as you please. It helps. Bonus points if you get a dog to croon with you due to your everlastingly beautiful tone quality.

2. Take a shot of guaifenesin followed by 8 ounces of water every four hours during days ten through seventeen of your cycle, to assist in cervical mucus consistency, because—gross did I really just write that? Anyway, Clomid will dry you out like a lush in a drunk tank. Isn't science neat?

3. Entertain yourself by coming up with every twin, triplet, and octuplet name combination you can think of. Write them down—you

may need them! If you need some help getting started, hey how's this? My great grandmother was named Eulah Faye, and her twin was named Beulah Mae. Gold, am I right?

4. You'll be bloated by the Clomid anyway, so I'd add a daily donut to your to-do list, so at least you can say you got there the fun way.

5. Come up with something extravagant to give yourself should the Clomid desert its post. This way you have something to look forward to, no matter what.

The second time I was infertile, it was 2012, and I wanted all of the tests. ALL OF THE TESTS. It's been two years and counting, and there is still no second baby to be seen. But I *have* had all the tests my little heart desired, lucky me. Just two, actually. And now we will discuss them.

1. THE BLOOD TEST

This test measures the age and viability of your eggs. Eggs are sort of crucial here. If your hormones are bad or if you're not ovulating regularly or if you're dealing with subpar swimmers, there's a lot you can do. But if your eggs aren't any good, you're mostly up a creek. My eggs are fine. Except for that two-week period where they weren't fine, because my OB is a nutcase. And so I decided to go for a second opinion at a very expensive fertility clinic. I'd waited in those waiting room chairs before in other clinics in other cities. Every waiting room chair looks exactly the same, all with the layers of pain and anticipation woven right into the upholstering. And I'd fought this fight before. I'd fought it and won, but I was starting to doubt I could do it again. As I considered the possibility of old, useless eggs, and what all that would mean, I asked myself, *Do I really want to do this? No more babies.* I could make that decision for myself. Or I could stay where I was and pay some specialist to tell me my OB was right, it was over. YOU ARE FINISHED. YOUR PARTS DON'T WORK. But I think I knew that wasn't the case, and so, do I fight that fight again? Or do I walk right out of that waiting room and never look back? I could choose to be complete, though I knew that I wouldn't be. I would always regret it if I didn't bring that last Holbrook home.

It was just then, that very precise instant, when in walked a dude wearing a velvet tuxedo.

Green velvet. At two o'clock in the afternoon. On a Tuesday.

He looked pretty sharp, I'll give him that. He strode across the room, took a seat in a chair against the wall, crossed one velvety leg over one very velvety knee, and then looked around the room like it was no big deal. But I swear the air had changed the second he walked in, and seeing him I just knew I could do it. I could bring that Holbrook home. How on earth could I not? How on earth could *anything* be impossible when at any time we are mere seconds from a velvet tuxedo?

Like I suspected, my eggs were *fine.* I shook the very expensive specialist's hand and made a mental note to both find a new OB *and* thank that velvet tuxedo for the shot of courage, but by the time I got back to the lobby, the velvet tuxedo was gone.

2. THE X-RAY TEST

Hysterosalpingogram. That's an X-ray test of your uterus and fallopian tubes that ascertains whether physical blockages are what's preventing fertilization. It's performed at a hospital.

First you sit in the waiting room for a while. All these waiting rooms, I tell you. You look at the faces of the other women here. You become aware that you're sitting with a lot of people's worries. They seep into your clothes from the cushions of the chair. You can see the worry in the walls; you can sense them in the air. Your worry and their worry and the worries of the people before you; somehow it's comforting. You listen to the conversations around you. One woman beat cancer, but now it's returned in her spine. She's awaiting an MRI. Another is here for a routine mammogram. Her eyes grow wide as the cancer survivor describes the surgeries she's had through the years. Two women are here in support of their friends, adding their worries to the mix. So many worries. And though I'm sad to admit it, I feel at home here among all these worries and questions. These women are my tribe. I am grateful for the smallness of my own in comparison, and so I send my worries in to mingle with the rest. We're all in this together, smiling gently at each other. We know we may all be okay, just as we know we all may not.

Your name, birth date, Social Security number, insurance information, more insurance information, the name of your parents' dog, and your favorite ride at Disneyland all goes into a plastic machine the size of a boulder. You glance at the screen and it reads, "Complaint: Infertility" in green lettering. You're hit with the significance. To see something that feels so enormous reduced to mere "complaint" is oddly refreshing. And then you are escorted to the women's locker room down the hall. You're handed a hospital gown and some instructions, and you go in to disrobe. Then you sit in another waiting area, this one a torn chair in a row of torn chairs in a very busy hallway, basking in the fluorescent lights

wearing just your socks and a hospital gown you accidentally put on backward.

Next, the X-ray room. There's a hutch on the left wall filled with medical supplies, its door slightly ajar. Inside are rows and rows of small plastic bottles of saline. You eye the paper covering on the bench.

"I prefer to work with the smaller speculum," the doctor is saying to the nurse while she sets up the equipment, and you try so hard not to crack a joke that your face scrunches up.

You're familiar with this part, the *This might be uncomfortable* part, and when he asks if you'll be all right you kind of roll your eyes. At this point your tolerance for pain and public indecency is a mile high. Repeated fertility treatments will do that to a girl.

It pinches, but it's not bad. The doctor stands up and brushes his hands on his pants and announces that he's off to get the specialist. He will be the one to push the button that inserts the dye. *This makes no sense,* you think. *It's just a button, why is a specialist necessary, and why couldn't he have been here already?* And then you're just lying there with this weird tube snaking out of you, and you feel like an unplugged lamp.

It occurs to you that there really is no dignity in being a woman, and just then the X-ray screen flickers on and there it is: You. The very you of you. It's weird, and reverent in a way. It feels like you're looking into something godly.

The feel of the dye is maybe the oddest sensation of your life. You hold your breath. When the little streaks of white show up on the screen, squiggling out of the dark space that signal your fallopian tubes, you breathe out a sigh of relief. You're working. You feel you've just accomplished something enormous. You take a photo of the screen with your smartphone. You high-five the nurse, because by now you two have become buds.

And then it's over.

You walk home with your head held high and your womanhood intact and a couple ibuprofen in your bag for later. Yessir! You, your perfectly unobstructed tubes, your once bad but now good-again eggs, you are on top of the world! You decide to take your follicles of promise on a celebratory tour of the neighborhood. To the bank to get some cash, to the West Elm to look at air plants, to Whole Foods to think about but then not buy a ten-dollar bottle of green juice. You and your uterus, you're a team. You've got this.

Two hours later the pain hits and you spend the rest of the night huddled on the couch with a hot water bottle. Because HSG tests are not messing around.

But then again, neither are we.

On Being the Boss of Your Poops

This morning Huck and I were having a very serious discussion about whether or not I was going to go down the stairs with him. I was telling him no, I was mid-mascara, and he was telling me yes, he needed to watch *Paw Patrol* ASAP. He pronounces it "pop the troll" and it's really pretty great, but sometimes the troll can wait. After a few rounds trying to convince me I was wrong, I knelt down on Huck's level, and I looked him in the eye, and I said, "Hey, who's the boss here?" Huck smiled a little devilishly and said "Mommy," one toddler finger pointing crookedly at me. // "But Mom," he continued, rather seriously. "I'm the boss of my poops." // That's my boy.

Potty training Huck was ridiculous. I mean, well, I didn't potty train Huck. Huck potty trained himself. It was kind of miraculous, really. I made up a little potty chart, I bought a bunch of Halloween, Christmas, and Chanukah stickers (gotta cover your bases), I canceled the recurring diaper order, I ordered the big-boy undies in bulk. And then, two hours of naked time later, he was just . . . potty trained. Not a single accident. It was bizarre, and it was wonderful. I continued to tend carefully to his potty chart for a few days, I suppose so I could feel useful on some level, but eventually the Chanukah stickers started popping up all over Huck's chest and shoulders so I shrugged and pulled it all down and life went on. Potty trained. Too easy?

Definitely too easy.

For his next trick, Huck up and stopped pooping. Cold turkey. Which is very common for freshly trained toddlers, according to a few nights of panicked Googling. He'd act like he had to go, he had this funny little dance he'd do when the poop came a-knockin', but when I'd gently suggest he might use the bathroom, he'd look at me like I was nuts and say, "No, Mom." As if it were the most obvious thing in the world.

This lasted for days, though it felt like years. For the sake of honesty in reporting, it was three days. One afternoon, mid-poop-strike, Huck admitted that he was a little afraid to poop, so I tried everything I could think of to help him feel more confident. I even tried forcing him on the potty and coaching him through it, like Lamaze. "That's right, breathe . . . and push!" But of course that never got us anywhere. And then one day in a fit of brilliance I declared, "Huck, you will just have to poop when you are ready to poop, and not a minute sooner. Because Huck, *you* are the boss of your poops."

And just like that we had our family motto.

Huck did eventually poop, is the good news, and he's been pooping like a champ ever since. And now, any time we come face to face with something big that we have zero control over, when all we can do is take care of ourselves and how we react in tough situations, we remind each other:

Hey. Be the boss of your poops.

I can't control much. I can't control the people I love, I can't control the people I don't love. I can't control the weather, I can't control even my *life*. Life is a control freak's worst nightmare. But I can control my poops. That's up to me. And anything else that falls under my jurisdiction, well, Imma be the boss of that too. I can do it when and where and however

I choose. Being the boss is cool like that.

I've always believed that every breath is a new chance to choose happiness. It's been my rallying cry for most of my adult life. Happiness is a choice. It isn't a place or a set of conditions. It is a fight that you take on and then take on again, every single day. You can't let yourself forget to choose to be happy. I mean, I let myself forget all the time, but that's not the point. The point is to remember the fight and get back in it the second you can.

I think so much of a rich life lies in being able to recognize the miracles and adventures as they are unfolding. Too many times we don't see these moments of our lives for what they are until after they're done. But there are miracles and adventures and moments around us always. The way the sun melts through the golden leaves on an autumn afternoon— that's an adventure. Morning French toast with chocolate chips on top that must be eaten with a "foon"—there's your miracle. Scattered crayons on the floor, stepping over plastic penguins in the shower—those are your moments. Being able to recognize them while they're happening, realizing that these are the moments you'll someday look back on with such fondness, and then letting those moments be as big as we can make them right now while we're in them—that's the trick. Those are your poops. We're living them now.

And as for me, I want to do them justice. I think that might be what life is about.

I've always believed that every breath is a new chance to choose happiness. It's been my rallying cry for most of my adult life. Happiness is a choice.

You know how when you're at Disneyland, and you're buying your tickets and they're playing the music from *Dumbo*, and you get on the line to go through the gates and you're all cheesy smiles and the ticket machine chirps at you and you get to walk in? Sometimes that's how I feel about restocking the soda. I got my kid strapped in his stroller and all of New York City at my feet. And I'm the boss of my poops.

Now that's an adventure.

Acknowledgments

Let this go down on permanent record as the hardest part of a book to write! Holy cow! Nothing would be possible without my husband. Thank you for being such a wonderful friend and partner and father and lover, for seeing so much more in me than what might actually be there, for cheering me on and believing in me, and thank you also for having such amazing red hair. I love you fiercely, Beebs.

Thank you to my readers for being so impossibly rad. I'm always floored by the caliber of women (and sometimes dudes) (but usually just chicks) that read my blog. I wrote this for every one of you; I wish you could all know what a huge blessing you have been in my life. Say *hi* when you see me next time—it is NOT creepy. If anyone is creepy it is *me* for putting pictures of myself on the Internet all the time.

Thank you Mom for loving me when I'm good, and thank you Dad for loving me when I'm ornery. Thank you Granny Goose for being so very *you*. I wish you were able to read this, you kooky old bat. To my sisters who are the world to me, and to Blake, my very first baby. And to Huck! For being EVERY-THING. I am so grateful to be your mom, thanks for taking it easy on me while I tried to juggle everything.

Thank you Abby Low, Lesley Unruh, Nicole Cordier, Bronson Bigelow, Dervla Kelly, Emma Kepley, Justin Hackworth, Isabelle Selby, and Rubi Jones for making me and my things look good.

Thank you to Holly Dolce, the world's greatest editor, hand-holder, pep-talker, and trash-talker, not to mention a really wonderful friend. To Nora Ephron and L.M. Montgomery, and Tina and Mindy and Amy, and to Meg Ryan, too, for my high-school haircut inspiration and for always being there in my DVD player when I had a bad day. Thank you. And of course, thank you, Al Gore, for inventing the Internet so I could make a fool of myself on it, and for giving me such an easy way to be contrary during my freshman year at BYU in 2000.

*Thank your,
ladies and gentlemen.
Thank your.*

Resources

*Half the battle in life
is knowing where to find
the good stuff. Below are
a few of my very favorite
spots to find inspiration.*

FOR MY HOME

West Elm / *westelm.com*
I love their Market Shop, where I like to get bath and laundry supplies, candles, and other miscellaneous items that remind me of camping gear.

Kaufmann Mercantile /
kaufmann-mercantile.com
For kitchen linens and pottery.

Urban Outfitters / *urbanoutfitters.com*
Their apartment section always has something inspiring.

Amazon / *amazon.com*
If it weren't for Amazon . . . just . . . something drastic.

Pendleton / *pendleton-usa.com*
A home is not a home until you have a Pendleton wool blanket stashed somewhere.

One King's Lane /
onekingslane.com
For a really great selection of Turkish rugs.

Ikea / *ikea.com*
Thank you, Ikea, for furnishing my home a zillion times over. Brandon makes me put everything together myself.

Hillside Schoolhouse /
hillsideschoolhouse.com
Proprietor Bronson Bigelow repurposes old iceboxes and found furniture into custom, one-of-a-kind pieces. His eye for balance is killer.

ABJ Glassworks / *abjglassworks.com*
For beautiful glass display pyramids and terrariums.

Pacific Coast / *pacificcoast.com*
For down duvets, the best in the market.

**Schoolhouse Electric
& Supply Co.** / *schoolhouseelectric.com*
For lighting, of course, but their general housewares selection is also spot on.

FOR MY CLOSET

rag & bone / *rag-bone.com*
For the perfect skinny jeans and really great sweaters.

Madewell / *madewell.com*
I usually pick up my denim here, and pretty much any shoe they ever sell I immediately drool over. Every season I do a quick Madewell sweep; they're my go-to brand. They also stock a fun mix of independent brands and designers that they love, and that I usually love, too.

Isabel Marant / *isabelmarant.com*
In my dreams . . .

Objects Without Meaning / *objectswithoutmeaning.com*
One of my favorites—I love that everything from the line is produced here in the US, and that they manage to strike that perfect balance between on-trend, edgy materials set against some really classic lines (or the other way around).

Hackwith Design House /
hackwithdesignhouse.com
Handmade, beautifully structured, one-of-a-kind pieces.

Barneys / *barneys.com*
For drooling.

Need Supply Co. / *needsupply.com*
For anything with a minimalist, edgy, feminine look.

Forestbound / *forestbound.com*
For beautiful handcrafted bags made from recycled leathers and army canvas.

Acne Studios / *acnestudios.com*
Makes the leather jacket of my dreams.

Alexander Wang / *alexanderwang.com*
Good source for slouchy tee shirts.

Steven Alan / *stevenalan.com*
I love to go to Steven Alan for their delicate jewelry and ultrasoft knitwear.

Everlane / *www.everlane.com*
For sweaters! Any and all Everlane sweaters are gold. They have the best affordable cashmere. I practically live in their seed-stitch box-cut sweaters from October through April. Plus, they have amazingly constructed basics.

Forever 21 / *forever21.com*
(Let's not kid ourselves.)

FOR MY FEET

Loeffler Randall / *loefflerrandall.com*
Killer shoes that are just laidback enough to look like you're not trying very hard.

H by Hudson / *hudsonshoes.com*
Ass-kicking boots.

Rachel Comey / *rachelcomey.com*
The Mars boot is such a classic and worth the investment. They're the only slight-heeled boots you'll ever need. Also, clogs!

Nina Z Clogs / *ninaznyc.com*
I know Nina and she is just the bee's knees.

Birkenstock / *birkenstock.com*
For feeling like a platypus (why do I love these so much?).

Bensimon / *www.bensimon.com*
The perfect summer sneaker.

Converse / *www.converse.com*
I buy a new pair of white All Star hi tops for fall every year.

FOR MY JEWELRY BOX

Littionary NYC / *littionary.com*
Sells the tiniest stud earrings you'll ever find.

Catbird / *catbirdnyc.com*
Good spot to find stacking rings.

Monocrafft / *monocrafft.com*
Really fantastic threaded earrings.

Love Adorned / *loveadorned.com*
Gorgeous dainty gold jewelry.

Timex / *timex.com*
Sporty watches that don't feel too sporty.

Casio / *casio.com*
I don't care who you are, a nerd watch is always appropriate.

FOR MY FACE & BODY

Aesop / *aesop.com*
For the heavy-duty skin creams.

Chanel / *chanel.com*
I just really love their mascara, especially Le Volume 10 in noir. It's one of those mascaras where I really didn't want it to be great, but then it was, really really great, and I was like, well, fine.

Kiehl's / *kiehls.com*
For tinted moisturizer.

Trader Joe's / *traderjoes.com*
Best organic coconut oil on planet earth.

Elma & Sana / *elma-sana.com*
For Moroccan rose water—an excellent toner

Le Labo / *lelabofragrances.com*
Their fragrances are all great, but Santal 33 is my favorite; a gorgeously rich, spicy, warm sandalwood, with seductively sweet undertones. It's somehow masculine and soft. I basically like to smell sweet like food, or spicy like a dude. With this one, I smell like both!

Sachajuan / *sachajuan.com*
The Ocean Mist Spray is a fantastic salt spray.

FOR MY HAIR

L'Oreal Paris Elnett Satin / *lorealparisusa.com*
The best hairspray known to man.

Kérastase / *kerastase-usa.com*
I can't help myself. I am just addicted to this shampoo and conditioner. Nutritive Bain Satin 2 shampoo and Lait Vital conditioner are my favorites.

Mason Pearson / *masonpearson.com*
The kind of brush that will make you feel like an old Hollywood glamour star

Days + Nights NYC / *www.su-juk.com*
For powder dry shampoo—the lavender scent is divine.

Lulu Organics / *luluorganics.com*
For powder dry shampoo that smells amazing.

Batiste / *batistehair.com*
Makes the best aerosol dry shampoos on the market.

FOR BRANDON

J.Crew / *jcrew.com*
Because obviously. Shopping here is a brainless way to pick up a few great button-downs per season. They sell the most comfortable, best-fitting merino wool sweaters.

Accompany / *accompanyus.com*
My favorite place to stock up on Ace & Jig, a really lovely clothing line run by two of my good friends.

Filson / *filson.com*
So he can feel like a lumberjack.

Izola / *izola.com*
This is a perfect spot for host/hostess gifts and stocking stuffers. Their soap sets and soap dishes are so great. Their dopp kits are my absolute favorite.

FOR HUCK

Zara Kids / *zara.com*
When in doubt, Zara will have it.

Gap Kids / *gap.com*
The girl's section, specifically. I buy their medium and dark wash skinny jeans. I may never buy my son a pair of pants intended for a boy ever again.

American Apparel / *americanapparel.net*
The bulk of Huck's wardrobe comes from American Apparel. It's just really great stuff.

Saltwater Sandals / *saltwater-sandals.com*
The best summer sandal.

Stokke / *stokke.com*
The best place to find baby gear that won't look atrocious in your living room.